English / Armharic Phrasebook (amh)

የእንግሊዝኛ / አማርኛ የአነጋገር መዝገበ ቃላት

(ye'inigilīzinya / āmarinya ye'ānegageri mezigebe k'alati)

John C. Rigdon

English / Amharic Dictionary

English / Amharic Phasebook

የእንግሊዝኛ / አማርኛ የአነጋገር መዝገበ ቃላት

(ye'inigilīzinya / āmarinya ye'ānegageri mezigebe k'alati)

1st Printing – MAY 2016 CS

© Copyright 2016. Eastern Digital Resources. All Rights Reserved. No part of this book may be reproduced by any means without the express written consent of the copyright holder.

© የቅጂ መብት 2016 በምሥራቅ ዲጂታል መርጃዎች. መብቱ በህግ የተጠበቀ ነው. ምንም የዚህ መጽሐፍ ክፍል የቅጂ መብት ባለቤቱ ለማቋቋምና በጽሑፍ ፈቃድ ሳያገኝ ማንኛውንም መንገድ ማባዛት የተከለከለ ነው.

© yek'ijī mebiti 2016 bemiširak'i dījītali merijawochi . mebitu behigi yetet'ebek'e newi. minimi yezīhi mets'iḥāfi kifili yek'ijī mebiti balebētu lemak'wak'wamina bets'iḥufi fek'adi sayagenyi maninyawinimi menigedi mabazati yetekelekele newi.

Published by:
Eastern Digital Resources
31 Bramblewood Dr. SW
Cartersville, Ga 30120 USA
http://www.wordsrus.info
EMAIL: Sales@wordsrus.info
Tel. (678) 739-9177

Contents

Introduction 10

A Guide to English Pronunciation 11

    The English Alphabet 12

    English Vowels 13

    Nouns 14

    Adjectives 17

    Determiners 20

    Verbs 21

    Adverbs 25

    How to Pronounce Dates and Numbers 37

    Linking Between Words 40

Amharic (አማርኛ) 43

    History 43

    Language 44

    Why Learn The Amharic Language? 45

    Writing system 46

    Punctuation 47

Numerals 47

Sample text in Amharic 48

Consonants 49

Useful phrases in Amharic 50

Amharic abugida (ፊደል) 59

Gemination 61

Punctuation 61

Grammar 62

Pronouns 63

Subject-verb agreement 63

Object pronoun suffixes 63

Possessive suffixes 65

Avarice ethaiopa ግርኛ Personalized ግርኛ ehtiopia Pronouns 67

Reflexive pronouns 68

Demonstrative pronouns 69

Amharic Demonstrative Pronouns 69

Nouns 70

Gender 70

Plural 71

Archaic forms 72

Definiteness 73

Accusative 74

Nominalization 75

Verbs 76

Conjugation 76

Gerund 76

Verbal use 76

Adverbial use 77

Adjectives 77

Nominal patterns 77

Denominalizing suffixes 78

Adjective noun complex 78

Dialects 79

Conversation 80

ንግግር   nigigiri 80

English / Amharic Dictionary

Animals 83

እንስሳት   inisisati 83

Transportation 85

መጓጓዣ   megwagwazha 85

Directions 86

አቅጣጫዎች   āk'it'ach'awochi 86

Places 87

ቦታዎች   botawochi 87

Clothing 88

ልብስ   libisi 88

Colors 89

ቀለማት   k'elemati 89

People 91

ሕዝብ   hizibi 91

Jobs 92

ስራዎች   sirawochi 92

Society 93

| ማኅበር mahิberi | 93 |

Art 94

ሥነ ጥበብ šine t'ibebi 94

Beverages 95

መጠጦች met'et'ochi 95

Food 96

ምግብ migibi 96

Home 98

መኖሪያ ቤት menorīya bēti 98

Electronics 99

ኤሌክትሮኒክስ ēlēkitironīkisi 99

Nature 100

ፍጥረት fit'ireti 100

Measurements 102

መመጠን memet'eni 102

Directions 103

አቅጣጫዎች āk'it'ach'awochi 103

Seasons 104

ወቅት	wek'iti	104

Numbers 105

ቁጥሮች	k'ut'irochi	105

Months 107

ወሮች	werochi	107

Days 108

ቀናት	k'enati	108

Time 109

ጊዜ	gīzē	109

Body 110

አካል	ākali	110

Medical 112

የሕክምና	yeḥikimina	112

Money 113

ገንዘብ	genizebi	113

Family 114

ቤተሰብ	bētesebi	114

የእንግሊዝኛ / አማርኛ የአነጋገር መዝገበ ቃላት   9

English / Amharic/ Transliteration 116

የአማርኛ / እንግሊዝኛ / በቅንቅ 140

bek'wanik'wa / ye'āmarinya / inigilīzinya 164

መጽሐፍ ቅዱስ ከ የተመረጡ ቁጥር 188

Selected Verses from the Bible 192

Sources Used 197

Introduction

This phrase book contains a guide to English pronunciation and Grammar, a guide to Amharic pronunciation and Grammar, sample phrases and sentences arranged by topic and a dictionary of 700 of the most commonly used words and phrases.

For pronunciation and definitions of the words in this book, see our website at

http://www.wordsrus.info

A Guide to English Pronunciation

English is not a phonetic language. It has borrowed many words from other languages and words are often not pronounced as they seem.

The sounds of English and the International Phonetic Alphabet:

http://www.antimoon.com/how/pronunc-soundsipa.htm

An excellent resource with videos for learning to pronounce English words;

http://rachelsenglish.com/

The English Alphabet

English Alphabet with Pronunciation

A a	B b	C c	D d	E e
[eɪ]	[biː]	[siː]	[diː]	[iː]

F f	G g	H h	I i	J j
[ef]	[dʒiː]	[eɪtʃ]	[aɪ]	[dʒeɪ]

K k	L l	M m	N n	O o
[keɪ]	[el]	[em]	[en]	[əʊ]

P p	Q q	R r	S s	T t
[piː]	[kjuː]	[aː]	[es]	[tiː]

U u	V v	W w		
[juː]	[viː]	[ˈdʌbəljuː]		

X x	Y y	Z z		
[eks]	[waɪ]	[zed/ziː]		

English Vowels

A

E

I

O

U

Y

Nouns

Nouns answer the questions "**What is it?**" and "**Who is it?**" They give names to things, people, and places.

Examples

- dog
- bicycle
- Mary
- girl
- beauty
- France
- world

In general there is no distinction between masculine, feminine in English nouns. However, gender is sometimes shown by different forms or different words when referring to people or animals.

Examples

Masculine	Feminine	Gender neutral
man	woman	person
father	mother	parent
boy	girl	child

የእንግሊዝኛ / አማርኛ የእነጋር መዝገበ ቃላት

Masculine	Feminine	Gender neutral
uncle	aunt	
husband	wife	spouse
actor	actress	
prince	princess	
waiter	waitress	server
rooster	hen	chicken
stallion	mare	horse

Many nouns that refer to people's roles and jobs can be used for either a masculine or a feminine subject, like for example *cousin, teenager, teacher, doctor, student, friend, colleague*

Examples

- Mary is my friend. She is a doctor.
- Peter is my cousin. He is a doctor.
- Arthur is my friend. He is a student.
- Jane is my cousin. She is a student.

It is possible to make the distinction for these neutral words by adding the words *male* or *female*.

Examples

- Sam is a female doctor.
- No, he is not my boyfriend, he is just a male friend.
- I have three female cousins and two male cousins.

Infrequently, nouns describing things without a gender are referred to with a gendered pronoun to show familiarity. It is also correct to use the gender-neutral pronoun (it).

Examples

- I love my car. **She** (the car) is my greatest passion.
- France is popular with **her** (France's) neighbours at the moment.
- I travelled from England to New York on the Queen Elizabeth; **she** (the Queen Elizabeth) is a great ship.

Adjectives

Adjectives describe the aspects of nouns. When an adjective is describing a noun, we say it is "modifying" it. Adjectives can:

Describe feelings or qualities

Examples

- He is a **lonely** man.
- They are **honest**.

Give nationality or origin

Examples

- I heard a **French** song.
- This clock is **German**.
- Our house is **Victorian**.

Tell more about a thing's characteristics

Examples

- That is a **flashy** car.
- The knife is **sharp**.

Tell us about age

Examples

- He's a **young** man.
- My coat is **old**.

Tell us about size and measurement

Examples

- John is a **tall** man.
- This film is **long**.

Tell us about color

Examples

- Paul wore a **red** shirt.
- The sunset was **crimson**.

Tell us what something is made of

Examples

- The table is **wooden**.
- She wore a **cotton** dress.

Tell us about shape

Examples

- I sat at a **round** table.
- The envelope is **square**.

Express a judgment or a value

Examples

- That was a **fantastic** film.
- Grammar is **complicated**.

Determiners

Determiners are words placed in front of a noun to make it clear what the noun refers to. Use the pages in this section to help you use English determiners correctly.

Determiners in English

- Definite article : the
- Indefinite articles : a, an
- Demonstratives: this, that, these, those
- Pronouns and possessive determiners : my, your, his, her, its, our, their
- Quantifiers : a few, a little, much, many, a lot of, most, some, any, enough
- Numbers : one, ten, thirty
- Distributives : all, both, half, either, neither, each, every
- Difference words : other, another
- Pre-determiners : such, what, rather, quite

Verbs

Selecting the correct verb tense and conjugating verbs correctly is tricky in English. Click on the verb tense to read more about how to form this tense and how it is used, or select a time to see the full list of tenses and references on that time.

Present Tenses in English	Examples
Simple present tense	They **walk** home.
Present continuous tense	They **are walking** home.

Past Tenses in English	
Simple past tense	Peter **lived** in China in 1965.
Past continuous tense	I **was reading** when she arrived.

Perfect Tenses in English	
Present perfect tense	I **have lived** here since 1987.

Present Tenses in English	Examples
Present perfect continuous	I **have been living** here for years.
Past perfect	We **had been** to see her several times before she visited us.
Past perfect continuous	He **had been watching** her for some time when she turned and smiled.
Future perfect	We **will have arrived** in the States by the time you get this letter.
Future perfect continuous	By the end of your course, you **will have been studying** for five years.
Future Tenses in English	
Simple future tense	They **will go** to Italy next week.
Future continuous tense	I **will be travelling** by train.

Conditional Tenses in English

Zero conditional	If ice **gets** hot it **melts**.
Type 1 conditional	If he **is** late I **will be** angry.
Type 2 conditional	If he **was** in Australia he **would be getting up** now.
Type 3 conditional	She **would have visited** me if she **had had** time.
Mixed conditional	I **would be playing** tennis if I **hadn't broken** my arm.

The -ing forms in English

Gerund	I like **swimming**.
Present participle	She goes **running** every morning.

Adverbs

Adverbs are a very broad collection of words that may describe how, where, or when an action took place. They may also express the viewpoint of the speaker about the action, the intensity of an adjective or another adverb, or several other functions. Use these pages about the grammar of adverbs in English to become more precise and more descriptive in your speaking and writing.

Adverbs modify, or tell us more about, other words. Usually adverbs modify verbs, telling us how, how often, when, or where something was done. The adverb is placed after the verb it modifies.

Examples

- The bus moved **slowly**.
- The bears ate **greedily**.
- The car drove **fast**.

Sometimes adverbs modify adjectives, making them stronger or weaker.

Examples

- You look **absolutely** fabulous!
- He is **slightly** overweight.
- You are **very** persistent.

Some types of adverbs can modify other adverbs, changing their degree or precision.

Examples

- She played the violin **extremely** well.
- You're speaking **too** quietly.
-

Adverbs of time

Adverbs of time tell us when an action happened, but also for how long, and how often.

Adverbs that tell us when

Adverbs that tell us when are usually placed at the end of the sentence.

Examples

- Goldilocks went to the Bears' house **yesterday**.
- I'm going to tidy my room **tomorrow**.
- I saw Sally **today**.
- I will call you **later**.
- I have to leave **now**.
- I saw that movie **last year**.

Putting an adverb that tells us when at the end of a sentence is a neutral position, but these adverbs can be put in other positions to give a different emphasis. All adverbs that tell us when can be placed at the beginning of the sentence to emphasize the time element. Some can also be put before the main verb in formal writing, while others cannot occupy that position.

የእንግሊዝኛ / አማርኛ የኣነጋገር መዝገበ ቃላት 27

Examples

- **Later** Goldilocks ate some porridge. (the time is important)
- Goldilocks **later** ate some porridge. (this is more formal, like a policeman's report)
- Goldilocks ate some porridge **later**. (this is neutral, no particular emphasis)

Adverbs that tell us for how long

Adverbs that tell us for how long are also usually placed at the end of the sentence.

Examples

- She stayed in the Bears' house **all day**.
- My mother lived in France **for a year**.
- I have been going to this school **since 1996**.

In these adverbial phrases that tell us for how long, *for* is always followed by an expression of duration, while *since* is always followed by an expression of a point in time.

Examples

- I stayed in Switzerland **for three days**.
- I am going on vacation **for a week**.
- I have been riding horses **for several years**.
- The French monarchy lasted **for several centuries**.
- I have not seen you **since Monday**.
- Jim has been working here **since 1997**.
- There has not been a more exciting discovery **since last century**.

Adverbs that tell us how often

Adverbs that tell us how often express the frequency of an action. They are usually placed before the main verb but after auxiliary verbs (such as *be, have, may, & must*). The only exception is when the main verb is "to be", in which case the adverb goes after the main verb.

Examples

- I **often** eat vegetarian food.
- He **never** drinks milk.
- You must **always** fasten your seat belt.
- I am **seldom** late.
- He **rarely** lies.

Many adverbs that express frequency can also be placed at either the beginning or the end of the sentence, although some cannot be. When they are placed in these alternate positions, the meaning of the adverb is much stronger.

Adverb that can be used in two positions	Stronger position	Weaker position
frequently	I visit France **frequently**.	I **frequently** visit France.
generally	**Generally**, I don't like spicy foods.	I **generally** don't like spicy foods.

Adverb that can be used in two positions	Stronger position	Weaker position
normally	I listen to classical music **normally**.	I **normally** listen to classical music.
occasionally	I go to the opera **occasionally**.	I **occasionally** go to the opera.
often	**Often**, I jog in the morning.	I **often** jog in the morning.
regularly	I come to this museum **regularly**.	I **regularly** come to this museum.
sometimes	I get up very early **sometimes**.	I **sometimes** get up very early.
usually	I enjoy being with children **usually**.	I **usually** enjoy being with children.

Some other adverbs that tell us how often express the exact number of times an action happens or happened. These adverbs are usually placed at the end of the sentence.

Examples

- This magazine is published **monthly**.
- He visits his mother **once a week**.
- I work **five days a week**.
- I saw the movie **seven times**.

Using Yet

Yet is used in questions and in negative sentences to indicate that something that has not happened or may not have happened but is expected to happen. It is placed at the end of the sentence or after *not*.

Examples

- Have you finished your work **yet**? (= simple request for information)
- No, not **yet**. (= simple negative answer)
- They haven't met him **yet**. (= simple negative statement)
- Haven't you finished **yet**? (= expressing surprise)

Using Still

Still expresses continuity. In positive sentences it is placed before the main verb and after auxiliary verbs such as *be, have, might, will*. If the main verb is *to be*, then place *still* after it rather than before. In questions, *still* goes before the main verb.

Examples

- She is **still** waiting for you.
- Jim might **still** want some.
- Do you **still** work for the BBC?
- Are you **still** here?
- I am **still** hungry.

Order of adverbs of time

If you need to use more than one adverb of time in a sentence, use them in this order:

1: how long 2: how often 3: when

Examples

- 1 + 2 : I work (1) **for five hours** (2) **every day**
- 2 + 3 : The magazine was published (2) **weekly** (3) **last year**.
- 1 + 3 : I was abroad (1) **for two months** (3) **last year**.
- 1 + 2 + 3 : She worked in a hospital (1) **for two days** (2) **every week** (3) **last year**.

Adverbs of place

Adverbs of place tell us where something happens. They are usually placed after the main verb or after the clause that they modify. Adverbs of place do not modify adjectives or other adverbs.

Examples

- John looked **around** but he couldn't see the monkey.
- I searched **everywhere** I could think of.
- I'm going **back** to school.
- Come **in**!
- They built a house **nearby**.
- She took the child **outside**.

Here and There

Here and *there* are common adverbs of place. They give a location relative to the speaker. With verbs of movement, *here* means "towards or with the speaker" and *there* means "away from, or not with the speaker".

Sentence	Meaning
Come here!	Come towards me.
The table is in here.	Come with me; we will go see it together.
Put it there.	Put it in a place away from me.
The table is in there.	Go in; you can see it by yourself.

Here and *there* are combined with prepositions to make many common adverbial phrases.

Examples

- What are you doing **up there**?
- Come **over here** and look at what I found!
- The baby is hiding **down there** under the table.
- I wonder how my driver's license got stuck **under here**.

Here and *there* are placed at the beginning of the sentence in exclamations or when emphasis is needed. They are followed by the verb if the subject is a noun or by a pronoun if the subject is a pronoun.

Examples

- **Here** comes the bus!
- **There** goes the bell!

- **There** it is!
- **Here** they are!

Adverbs of place that are also prepositions

Many adverbs of place can also be used as prepositions. When used as prepositions, they must be followed by a noun.

Word	Used as an adverb of place, modifying a verb	Used as a preposition
around	The marble **rolled around** in my hand.	I am wearing a necklace **around my neck**.
behind	Hurry! You are **getting behind**.	Let's hide **behind the shed**.
down	Mary **fell down**.	John made his way carefully **down the cliff**.
in	We decided to **drop in** on Jake.	I dropped the letter **in the mailbox**.
off	Let's **get off** at the next stop.	The wind blew the flowers **off the tree**.
on	We **rode on** for several	Please put the books **on**

Word	Used as an adverb of place, modifying a verb	Used as a preposition
over	more hours. He **turned over** and went back to sleep.	the table. I think I will hang the picture **over my bed**.

Adverbs of place ending in -where

Adverbs of place that end in -where express the idea of location without specifying a specific location or direction.

Examples

- I would like to go **somewhere** warm for my vacation.
- Is there **anywhere** I can find a perfect plate of spaghetti around here?
- I have **nowhere** to go.
- I keep running in to Sally **everywhere**!

Adverbs of place ending in -wards

Adverbs of place that end in -wards express movement in a particular direction.

Examples

- Cats don't usually walk **backwards**.
- The ship sailed **westwards**.
- The balloon drifted **upwards**.

- We will keep walking **homewards** until we arrive.

Be careful: *Towards* is a preposition, not an adverb, so it is always followed by a noun or a pronoun.

Examples

- He walked **towards the car.**
- She ran **towards me.**

Adverbs of place expressing both movement & location

Some adverbs of place express both movement & location at the same time.

Examples

- The child went **indoors.**
- He lived and worked **abroad.**
- Water always flows **downhill.**
- The wind pushed us **sideways.**

የእንግሊዝኛ / አማርኛ የአነጋገር መዝገበ ቃላት

How to Pronounce Dates and Numbers[1]

Dates
In English, we can say dates either with the day before the month, or the month before the day:
"The first of January" / **"January the first"**.

Remember to use ordinal numbers for dates in English.
(The first, the second, the third, the fourth, the fifth, the twenty-second, the thirty-first etc.)

Years
For years up until 2000, separate the four numbers into two pairs of two:
1965 = **"nineteen sixty-five"**
1871 = **"eighteen seventy-one"**
1999 = **"nineteen ninety-nine"**

For the decade 2001 – 2010, you say "two thousand and —-" when speaking British English:
2001 = **"two thousand and one"**
2009 = **"two thousand and nine"**

However, from 2010 onwards you have a choice.
For example, 2012 can be either **"two thousand and twelve"** or **"twenty twelve"**.

---

[1] Excerpted from http://www.english-at-home.com/pronunciation/saying-dates-and-numbers-in-english/

Large numbers
Divide the number into units of hundreds and thousands:
400,000 = "**four hundred thousand**" (no s plural)

If the number includes a smaller number, use "and" in British English:
450,000 = "**four hundred and fifty thousand**"
400,360 = "**four hundred thousand and three hundred and sixty**"

Fractions, ratios and percentages
½ = "**one half**"
1/3 = "**one third**"
¼ = "**one quarter**"
1/5 = "**one fifth**"
1/ 6 = "**one sixth**"
3/5 = "**three fifths**"

1.5% = "**one point five percent**"
0.3% = "**nought / zero point three percent**"

2:1 = "**two to one**"

Saying 0
Depending on the context, we can pronounce zero in different ways:
2-0 (football) = "**Two nil**"
30 – 0 (tennis) = "**Thirty love**"
604 7721 (phone number) = "**six oh four…**"
0.4 (a number) = "**nought point four**" or "**zero point four**"
0C (temperature) = "**zero degrees**"

Talking about calculations in English
+ (**plus**)

= (equals / makes)
2 + 1 = 3 ("two plus one equals / makes three")
− (minus / take away)
5 − 3 = 2 ("five minus three equals two" / "five take away three equals two")
x (multiplied by / times)
2 x 3 = 6 ("two multiplied by three equals six" / "two times three equals six")
/ (divided by)
6 / 3 = 2 ("six divided by three equals two")

Linking Between Words [2]

When you listen to spoken English, it very often sounds smooth, rather than staccato. One of the ways we achieve this is to link sounds between words.

Using a /r/ sound

For example, we use a /r/ sound between two vowel sounds (when one word ends with a vowel sound of 'uh' (as in the final sound of banana); 'er' (as in the final sound of murder); and 'or' (as in the final sound of or). The /r/ sound happens when the next word starts with a vowel.

A matter of opinion = "A matte – rof opinion"

Murder is a crime = "Murde – ris a crime"

For example = "Fo – rexample".

Using a /w/ sound

We use a /w/ sound when the first word ends in a 'oo' sound (as in you); or an 'oh' sound (as in no) or an 'ow' sound (as in now)

---

[2] Excerpted from http://www.english-at-home.com/pronunciation/linking-between-words/

Who are your best friends? = "Who - ware - your ....."

No you don't = "No - wyou don't"

Now I know = "No - wI - know"

Using a /j/ sound

If you say the words "I" and "am" quickly, the sound between is a /ya/ sound. You can probably feel the sound at the back of your mouth, as the bottom of your mouth comes up to meet the top. The /j/ sound can link words which end with an /ai/ sound (I) or an /ey/ sound (may).

I am English = I - yam English

May I go? = May - jI go?

Consonant and vowel

When one word ends with a consonant (and the next begins with a vowel sound) use the final consonant to link.

An + apple sounds like a - napple.

Don't add an extra vowel after that consonant. So it's a - napple, rather than a - n - a apple.

Here are some more examples of consonants linking to vowels:

At all = "A - tall"

Speak up = "Spea - kup"

Right away = "Righ - taway"

Leave it = "Lea - vit"

School again = "Schoo - lagain"

Amharic (አማርኛ)

History

The Amharic language is a Semitic language that is used primarily in North Central Ethiopia. It is spoken mostly by the Amhara, an ethnic group in the central highlands of Ethiopia, but has also been adopted by many groups unrelated to this area.

In terms of script, the Amharic language does not use a Romanized western script, but instead is written using Ge'ez, an alphabet adapted to write primarily Semitic languages. It is a more ornate way of communicating language, much more so than the Roman alphabet.

Similar to many languages, Amharic uses gendered language when describing most things, but more interesting than that, male and female nouns and pronouns can also be used to convey certain emotions. For example, female pronouns can be used to indicate that something is petite or delicate, or even to express sympathy. This language is a complex and beautiful one.

Popularity

The Amharic language is the official language of Ethiopia, and is spoken in many specific regions such as Addis Ababa, the Amhara Region, the Benishangul-Gumuz Region, the Dire Dawa Administrative council, and the Gambela Region. It does not share importance with any other languages.

Due to the rise in emigration, Amharic has now been included in various computer software packages, with public service organizations making a point of including Amharic as another vital language to include in their translation and interpretation services. It is a language that is still spoken by some 2.7 million emigrants. These Amharic speakers have significant numbers in Canada, the US, and Sweden. It has been the working language of government, the military, and the Ethiopian Orthodox Tewahedo Church throughout medieval and modern times.

There is also an increasing body of literature written in Amharic. This literature is beginning to span many genres, and includes various novels, poems, proverbs, government records, educational books, religious books, tech. manuals, medical discussions, etc, etc.

Language

Since the Amharic language uses wholly its own language, it is relatively difficult to translate the Amharic language into Roman characters. There is no one way to do this, so as with the Indian language, for example, the translations have to be made aurally and transcribed as they are heard.

Amharic uses an alphasyllabary, or abugida, which is a writing system based on the pairing of consonants with vowels. Every character in the Amharic language represents a consonant and vowel pairing, which can make it a little easier to translate. Many of the symbols have a very similar look to each other, but this is partly because the consonants look very different from each other, while the vowels are rather supplemental. Because of this, words can be identified by native speakers often by their consonants alone.

The Amharic language also has a small number of differentiations between who you are speaking to, and their gender, in terms of personal pronouns. Similar to English, the Amharic language also shows positions in terms of demonstrative pronouns, such as "these" and "those". There is no neutral pronoun, but only feminine or masculine ones.

Why Learn The Amharic Language?

Amharic is the second most spoken Semitic language in the whole world. Arabic is the only Semitic language that can top this one, so if you're looking to learn your second, third, or even first Semitic language, then Amharic is at the top of the list.

The language itself, when written, is very beautiful. There is no singular way to translate the Amharic language into Roman lettering, so when one learns Amharic, it is necessary to get to grips with the written language just as much as the spoken language. This might be difficult, but the rewards are surely greater when one has to pour more effort into an endeavor.

If you are interested in music, particularly reggae, then Amharic would be a fascinating language to learn. Some Rastafarians learn the Amharic language voluntarily as a second language, as it is considered to be a sacred language, with many reggae songs using the Amharic language as the primary language of communication.

Amharic is a Semitic language and the national language of Ethiopia (ኢትዮጵያ). The majority of the 25 million or so speakers of Amharic can be found in Ethiopia, but there are also speakers in a number of other countries, particularly Eritrea (ኤርትራ), Canada, the USA and Sweden.

The name Amharic (አማርኛ - amarəñña) comes from the district of Amhara (አማራ) in nortern Ethiopia, which is thought to be the historic centre of the language.

Writing system

Amharic is written with a version of the Ge'ez script known as ፊደል (Fidel). There are a number of ways to transliterate Amharic into the Latin alphabet, including one developed by Ernst Hammerschmidt, the EAE Transliteration system, developed by Encyclopaedia Aethiopica, and the BGN/PCGN* system, which was designed for use in romanizing names written in Amharic characters and adopted by the UN in 1967.

*BGN = Board on Geographic Names (USA)
PCGN = The Permanent Committee on Geographical Names for British Official Use

More details:
http://www.pcgn.org.uk/Romanisation_systems.htm

Other syllables

ቷ	ቿ	ቿ	ቸ	ኋ	ኌ	ኍ	ኲ	ኳ	ኴ	ኵ	ጒ
kʷi	kʷa	kʷe	kʷɛ	hʷi	hʷa	hʷe	hʷɛ	kʷi	kʷa	kʷe	kʷɛ	gʷi

ጓ	ጔ	ጕ	ሏ	ቧ	ዟ	ጧ	ማ	ቷ	ዧ	ጯ	ሯ	ጯ
gʷa	gʷe	gʷɛ	lʷa	bʷa	zʷa	tʼʷa	mʷa	tʷa	ʒʷa	tʃʼʷa	rʷa	tʃʷa

ጿ	ጿ	ሷ	ኗ	ዷ	ፏ	ሿ	ኟ	ሯ	ሟ	ዿ	ኧ
dʒʷa	tsʼʷa	sʷa	nʷa	dʷa	fʷa	ʃʷa	ɲʷa	rʲa	mʲa	fʲa	ʔɛ

Punctuation

፣	።	፡	፤	፥	፧
comma	full stop / period	colon	semi-colon	preface colon	question mark (no longer used)

Numerals

These numerals developed from the Greek alphabet, possibly via Coptic.

፩	፪	፫	፬	፭	፮	፯	፰	፱	፲
አንዱ	ሁለት	ሶስት	አራት	አምስት	ስድስት	ሰባት	ስምንት	ዘጠኝ	አስር
and	hulätt	sost	aratt	amməst	səddəst	säbatt	səmmənt	zäṭäññ	assər
1	2	3	4	5	6	7	8	9	10

፳	፴	፵	፶	፷	፸	፹	፺	፻	፼
ሃያ	ሳላሳ	አርባ	ሃምሳ	ስልሳ	ስባ	ሰማንያ	ዘጠና	መቶ	ሺ
haya	sälasa	arba	hamsa	səlsa	säba	sämaña	zäṭena	mäto	ši
20	30	40	50	60	70	80	90	100	1000

English / Amharic Dictionary

Sample text in Amharic

የሰው : ልጅ : ሁሉ : ሲወለድ : ነጻና : በክብርና : በመብትም :
እኩልነት : ያለው : ነው : የተፈጥሮ : የማስተዋልና : ሕሊናው :
ስላለው : አንዱ : ሌላውን : በወንድማማችነት : መንፈስ :
መመልከት : የገባዋል ።

Transliteration (BGN/PCGN system)

yäsäw ləǧ hulu siwäläd näs'ana bäkəbərəna bämäbətəm
'əkulənät yaläw näw yätäfäpəro yämasətäwaləna həlinaw
səlaläw 'änədu lelawən bäwänədəmamačənät mänəfəs
mämäləkät yägäbawal.

Consonants[3]

		Bilabial	Alveolar	Palatal	Velar	Glottal
Nasal		m	n	ɲ (ñ)		
Plosive	voiceless	p	t		k	ʔ (')
	voiced	b	d		g	
	ejective	p' (p̣)	t' (ṭ)		k' (q)	
Affricate	voiceless			tʃ (č)		
	voiced			dʒ (ǧ)		
	ejective		ts' (ṣ)	tʃ' (č̣)		
Fricative	voiceless	f	s	ʃ (š)		h
	voiced	v*	z	ʒ (ž)		
Approximant			l	j (y)	w	
Rhotic			r			

* - Only in words borrowed from English and other languages

---

[3] Hayward, Katrina; Hayward, Richard J. (1999). "Amharic". *Handbook of the IPA*. Cambridge: Cambridge University Press. pp. 44-50.

Useful phrases in Amharic

A collection of useful phrases in Amharic, a Semitic language spoken in Ethiopia and Eritrea.

Key to abbreviations: inf = informal, frm = formal, >m = said to men, >f = said to women, pl = said to more than one person.

English	አማርኛ (Amharic)
Welcome	እንኳን ደህና መጣህ። (ənkwan dähna mättah) m እንኳን ደህና መጣሽ። (ənkwan dähna mättaš) f
Hello (General greeting)	ሰላም። (sälam) [peace] - inf ታዲያስ። (tadyass) - inf [how is it?] - inf ጤና ይስጥልኝ። (ṭenaisṭəlləň) >frm [may he (God) give you health on my behalf]
How are you?	እንደምን አለህ፤ (əndämən alläh?) >m እንደምን አለሽ፤ (əndämən alläš?) >f እንደምን አላችሁ፤ (əndämən allaččhu?) - pl
Reply to 'How are you?'	ደህና ነኝ። (dähna näň)
Long time no see	ረጅም ጊዜ ከተለያየን። (räǧǧim gize

	kätäläyayän)
What's your name?	ስምህ ማን ነው፧ (səməh man näw?) >m ስምሽ ማን ነው፧ (səməš man näw?) >f የእርስዎ ስም ማን ነው፧ (yärswo səm man näw?) >frm
My name is ...	የኔ ስም... ነው (yäne səm ... näw) ስሜ ... ነው። (səme ___ näw)
Where are you from?	ከየት ነህ፧ (käyät näh?) >m ከየት ነሽ፧ (käyät näš?) >f ከየት ኖት፧ (käyät not?) >frm አንተ ከየት ነህ፧ (antä käyät näh?) >m አንቺ ከየት ነሽ፧ (anchi käyät näš?) >f እርስዎ ከየት ኖት፧ (ərswo käyät not?) >frm
I'm from ...	እኔ ከ ... ነኝ። (əne kä ... näñ) ከ ... ነኝ። (kä ... näñ)
Pleased to meet you	ስለተዋወቅን ደስ ብሎኛል (səlätäwawäqən däs bəloññall)
Good morning (Morning greeting)	እንደምን አደርክ? (əndämən addärk?) >m እንደምን አደርሽ? (əndämən addärš?) >f እንደምን አደሩ? (əndämən addäru?) >frm [*how did you pass the night?*]
Good afternoon (Afternoon greeting)	እንደምን ዋልክ? (i'ndemin walik?) - m እንደምን ዋልሽ? (i'ndemin walish?) - f እንደምን ዋሉ (i'ndemin walu) - frm [*how did you spend the day?*]

Good evening (Evening greeting)	አንደምን አመሽህ? (əndämən amäššäh?) >m ምሽቱን እንዴት አሳለፍከው? (məššətun əndet asalläfkäw?) >m አንደምን አመሽሽ? (əndämən amäššäš?) >f ምሽቱን እንዴት አሳለፍሽው? (məššətun əndet asalläfšəw?) >f አንደምን አመሹ? (əndämən amäššu?) >frm [*how did you spend the evening?*]
Good night	ደህና እደር (dähna där) >m ደህና እደሪ (dähna däri) >f ደህና እደሩ (dähna däru) >frm/pl
Goodbye (Parting phrases)	ቻው (chaw) - inf ደህና ሁን (dähna hun) - m ደህና ሁኚ (dähna hunyi) - f ደህና ሁኑ (dähna hunu) - pl
Good luck	መልካም እድል (mälkam əddəl) - inf
Cheers! Good Health! (*Toasts used when drinking*)	ለጤናችን (läṭenaččən) ለፍቅራችን (läfəqraččən) ለጓደኛነታችን (lägwadäňňannätaččən)
Have a nice day	መልካም ቀን። (mälkam qän) መልካም ቀን ይሁንልህ። (mälkam qän yəhunəlləh) >m መልካም ቀን ይሁንልሽ። (mälkam qän yəhunəlləš) >f መልካም ቀን ይሁንላችሁ። (mälkam qän yəhunəllaččhu) - pl

Bon appetit / Have a nice meal	ብላ (bəla) - *eat!* >m ብዪ (biy) - *eat!* >f ብሉ (bəlu) - *eat!* - pl መልካም ምግብ (mälkam məgəb) - *good feasting*
Bon voyage / Have a good journey	መልካም ጉዞ። (mälkam guzo) መልካም ጉዞ ይሁንልህ። (mälkam guzo yəhunəlləh) >m መልካም ጉዞ ይሁንልሽ። (mälkam guzo yəhunəlləš) >f መልካም ጉዞ ይሁንላችሁ። (mälkam guzo yəhunəllaččhu) - pl
I understand	ገባኝ (gäbbañ) - *it entered me*
I don't understand	አልገባኝም (algäbbañem) - *it didn't enter me*
I don't know	አላውቅም (alawqəm)
Please speak more slowly	እባክህ ቀስ ብለህ ተናገር። (əbakəh qässə bəlläh tänagär) >m እባክሽ ቀስ ብለሽ ተናገሪ። (əbakəš qässə bəlläš tänagäri) >f እባካችሁ ቀስ ብላችሁ ተናገሩ። (əbakaččhu qässə bəlläččhu tänagäru) pl
Please say that again	እባክህ ያልከውን ድገምልኝ። (əbakəh yalkäwn dəgäməlləñ) >m እባክሽ ያልሽውን ድገሚልኝ። (əbakəš yalššəwn dəgämilləñ) >f

Please write it down	እባክሽ ያላችሁትን ድገሚልኝ። (əbakaččhu yalaččhutən dəgäməlləñ pl
Do you speak Amharic?	አማርኛ ትችላለህ? (amariňňa təčəlalläh) >m አማርኛ ትችያለሽ? (amariňňa təčiyalläš) >f አማርኛ ትችያላችሁ? (amariňňa təčəlallaččhu) pl
Yes, a little (*reply to 'Do you speak ...?'*)	አዎ፣ ትንሽ (aw tənəš)
How do you say ... in Amharic?	
Excuse me	ይቅርታ (yəqərta) - *forgivness*
How much is this?	ስንት ነው ዋጋው፤ (sənttə näw wagaw?)
Sorry	አዝናለሁ (azənallähw)- *I am sorrowful*
Please	እባከህ (əbakəh) - m እባከሽ (əbakəš) - f እባከዎን (əbakown) - frm - *I beg of you*
Thank you	አመሰግናለሁ (amäsäggänallähw) - *I praise you* በጣም አመሰግናለሁን (bätam amäsäggänallähun)

Reply to thank you	ምንም አይደለም (mənəm aydälläm) - *it is nothing* ችግር የለም (čəggər yälläm) - *there is no problem*
Where's the toilet?	ሽንት ቤት የት ነው? (šəntə bet yätə näw) - inf መጸዳጃ ክፍል የት ነው? (mäs'ädaǧǧa kəfl yätə näw) - frm
This gentleman will pay for everything	ለሁሉም ይህ ሰውየ ይከፍላል። (lähulum yəh säwye yəkäflall)
This lady will pay for everything	ለሁሉም ይህች ሴትዮ ትከፍላለች። (lähulum yəč setyo təkäflalläč)
Would you like to dance with me?	ከኔ ጋር መደነስ ትፈልጋለህ? (käne gar mädänäs təfälləgalläh?) >m ከኔ ጋር መደነስ ትፈልጊያለሽ? (käne gar mädänäs təfälləgiyalläš?) >f
I like you (as a friend)	እወድሃለሁ። (əwäddəhallähw) >m እወድሻለሁ። (əwäddəšallähw) >f
I love you	አፈቅርሻለሁ። (əfäqrəšallähw) >m አፈቅርሃለሁ። (əfäqrəhallähw) >f
Get well soon	ምህረቱን ያምጣልህ። (məhärätun yamṭalləh) >m ምህረቱን ያምጣልሽ። (məhärätun yamṭalləš) >f (*may his (God's) mercy come for you*)

Go away!	ሂድ! (hid) >m ሂጂ! (hiǧǧi) >f ሂዱ! (hidu) - pl
Leave me alone!	ለቀቅ አርገኝ። (läqäq arrəgäñ) >m ለቀቅ አርጊኝ። (läqäq arrəgiñ) >f
Help!	እርዳኝ! (ərdañ!) >m እርጂኝ! (ərǧǧiñ!) >f እርዱኝ! (ərduñ!) - pl
Fire!	እሳት! (əsat!)
Stop!	ቁም! (qum) >m ቁሚ! (qumi) >f
Call the police!	ፖሊስ ጥራ። (polis ṭərra!) >m ፖሊስ ጥሪ ። (polis ṭərri!) >f ፖሊስ ጥሩ ። (polis ṭərru!) - pl
Christmas and New Year greetings	እንኳን አደረሰህ (ənkwan adärräsäh) >m እንኳን አደረሰሽ (ənkwan adärräsäš) >f እንኳን አደረሱ (ənkwan adärräsu) - frm እንኳን አደረሳችሁ (ənkwan adärräsaččhu) - pl [even you have ushered in (the holiday)!] እንኳን አብረው አደረሰን (ənkwan abräw adärräsän) [reply - even we have ushered in together!]

Easter greetings	መልካም ፋሲካ (mälkam fasika)
Birthday greetings	መልካም ልደት (mälkam lədät)
One language is never enough	አንድ ቋንቋ ብቻ በቂ አይደለም (and qwanqa bəča bäqi aydälläm)
My hovercraft is full of eels Why this phrase?	የኔ ማንዣበቢያ መኪና በዓሣዎች ተሞልቷል (yäne manžabäbia mäkina bä'asawoch tämoltwal) - ["fish"] የኔ ማንዣበቢያ መኪና በእባቦች ተሞልቷል (yäne manžabäbia mäkina bä'əbaboch tämoltwal) - ["snakes"] (*there is no word for eels in Amharic*)

The Amharic script is an abugida, and the graphs of the Amharic writing system are called fidel. Each character represents a consonant+vowel sequence, but the basic shape of each character is determined by the consonant, which is modified for the vowel. Some consonant phonemes are written by more than one series of characters: /ʔ/, /s/, /s'/, and /h/ (the last one has four distinct letter forms). This is because these fidel originally represented distinct sounds, but phonological changes merged them. The citation form for each series is the consonant+ä form, i.e. the first column of the fidel. A font that supports Ethiopic, such as GF Zemen Unicode, is needed to see fidel on typical modern computer systems.

የእንግሊዝኛ / አማርኛ የአነጋገር መዝገበ ቃላት

Amharic abugida (ፊደል) [4]

The BGN/PCGN Amharic romanization system and the EAE Transliteration system are shown on the left of each column. Where there are two transliterations, the one of the right is the EAE one. IPA transcriptions are given under each syllable.

The syllables with the vowel transliterated as (i) are pronounced [ə], except in final position when the vowel is not pronounced.

---

[4] http://www.omniglot.com/writing/amharic.htm

English / Amharic Dictionary

		a/ā [a/ɛ]	u [u]	i [i]	a [a]	e [e]	ə [i]	o [o/ɔ]			a/ā [a/ɛ]	u [u]	i [i]	a [a]	e [e/ɛ]	(ə) [i/ʉ]	o [o/ɔ]
h [h]		ሀ ha	ሁ hu	ሂ hi	ሃ ha	ሄ he	ህ h(i)	ሆ ho	h/k [h]		ኀ hɛ	ኁ hu	ኂ hi	ኃ ha	ኄ he	ኅ h(i)	ኆ ho
l [l]		ለ lɛ	ሉ lu	ሊ li	ላ la	ሌ le	ል l(i)	ሎ lo	w [w]		ወ wɛ	ዉ wu	ዊ wi	ዋ wa	ዌ we	ው w(ʉ)	ዎ wo
h/ḥ [h]		ሐ ha	ሑ hu	ሒ hi	ሓ ha	ሔ he	ሕ h(i)	ሖ ho	ʼ/ʕ [ʔ]		ዐ ʔa	ዑ ʔu	ዒ ʔi	ዓ ʔa	ዔ ʔe	ዕ ʔi	ዖ ʔo
m [m]		መ mɛ	ሙ mu	ሚ mi	ማ ma	ሜ me	ም m(i)	ሞ mo	z [z]		ዘ zɛ	ዙ zu	ዚ zi	ዛ za	ዜ ze	ዝ z(i)	ዞ zo
s/ś [s]		ሠ sɛ	ሡ su	ሢ si	ሣ sa	ሤ se	ሥ s(i)	ሦ so	zh/ž [ʒ]		ዠ ʒɛ	ዡ ʒu	ዢ ʒi	ዣ ʒa	ዤ ʒe	ዥ ʒ(i)	ዦ ʒo
r [r]		ረ rɛ	ሩ ru	ሪ ri	ራ ra	ሬ re	ር r(i)	ሮ ro	y [j]		የ jɛ	ዩ ju	ዪ ji	ያ ja	ዬ je	ይ j(i)	ዮ jo
s [s]		ሰ sɛ	ሱ su	ሲ si	ሳ sa	ሴ se	ስ s(i)	ሶ so	d [d]		ደ dɛ	ዱ du	ዲ di	ዳ da	ዴ de	ድ d(i)	ዶ do
sh/š [ʃ]		ሸ ʃɛ	ሹ ʃu	ሺ ʃi	ሻ ʃa	ሼ ʃe	ሽ ʃ(i)	ሾ ʃo	j/ǧ [dʒ]		ጀ dʒɛ	ጁ dʒu	ጂ dʒi	ጃ dʒa	ጄ dʒe	ጅ dʒ(i)	ጆ dʒo
k'/q [k']		ቀ k'ɛ	ቁ k'u	ቂ k'i	ቃ k'a	ቄ k'e	ቅ k'(i)	ቆ k'o	g [g]		ገ gɛ	ጉ gu	ጊ gi	ጋ ga	ጌ ge	ግ g(i)	ጎ go
qh [ʁ']		ቐ ʁ'ɛ	ቑ ʁ'u	ቒ ʁ'i	ቓ ʁ'a	ቔ ʁ'e	ቕ ʁ'(i)	ቖ ʁ'o	t'/ṭ [t']		ጠ t'ɛ	ጡ t'u	ጢ t'i	ጣ t'a	ጤ t'e	ጥ t'(i)	ጦ t'o
b [b]		በ bɛ	ቡ bu	ቢ bi	ባ ba	ቤ be	ብ b(i)	ቦ bo	ch'/č̣ [tʃ']		ጨ tʃ'ɛ	ጩ tʃ'u	ጪ tʃ'i	ጫ tʃ'a	ጬ tʃ'e	ጭ tʃ'(i)	ጮ tʃ'o
t [t]		ተ tɛ	ቱ tu	ቲ ti	ታ ta	ቴ te	ት t(i)	ቶ to	p'/ṗ [p']		ጰ p'ɛ	ጱ p'u	ጲ p'i	ጳ p'a	ጴ p'e	ጵ p'(i)	ጶ p'o
ch/č [tʃ]		ቸ tʃɛ	ቹ tʃu	ቺ tʃi	ቻ tʃa	ቼ tʃe	ች tʃ(i)	ቾ tʃo	ts'/ṣ [ts]		ጸ ts'ɛ	ጹ ts'u	ጺ ts'i	ጻ ts'a	ጼ ts'e	ጽ ts'(i)	ጾ ts'o
h/ḫ [h]		ኀ ha	ኁ hu	ኂ hi	ኃ ha	ኄ he	ኅ h(i)	ኆ ho	ts'/ṣ́ [ts]		ፀ ts'ɛ	ፁ ts'u	ፂ ts'i	ፃ ts'a	ፄ ts'e	ፅ ts'(i)	ፆ ts'o
n [n]		ነ nɛ	ኑ nu	ኒ ni	ና na	ኔ ne	ን n(i)	ኖ no	f [f]		ፈ fɛ	ፉ fu	ፊ fi	ፋ fa	ፌ fe	ፍ f(i)	ፎ fo
ny/ñ [ɲ]		ኘ ɲɛ	ኙ ɲu	ኚ ɲi	ኛ ɲa	ኜ ɲe	ኝ ɲ(i)	ኞ ɲo	p [p]		ፐ pɛ	ፑ pu	ፒ pi	ፓ pa	ፔ pe	ፕ p(i)	ፖ po
ʼ/ʔ [ʔ]		አ ʔa	ኡ ʔu	ኢ ʔi	ኣ ʔa	ኤ ʔe	እ ʔi	ኦ ʔo	v [v]		ቨ vɛ	ቩ vu	ቪ vi	ቫ va	ቬ ve	ቭ v(i)	ቮ vo
k [k]		ከ kɛ	ኩ ku	ኪ ki	ካ ka	ኬ ke	ክ k(i)	ኮ ko									

Gemination

As in most other Ethiopian Semitic languages, gemination is contrastive in Amharic. That is, consonant length can distinguish words from one another; for example, alä 'he said', allä 'there is'; yəmätall 'he hits', yəmmättall 'he is hit'. Gemination is not indicated in Amharic orthography, but Amharic readers typically do not find this to be a problem. This property of the writing system is analogous to the vowels of Arabic and Hebrew or the tones of many Bantu languages, which are not normally indicated in writing. Ethiopian novelist Haddis Alemayehu, who was an advocate of Amharic orthography reform, indicated gemination in his novel Fəqər Əskä Mäqabər by placing a dot above the characters whose consonants were geminated, but this practice is rare.

Punctuation

Punctuation includes the following:

፡ section mark፡ word separator። full stop (period)፣ comma፤ semicolon፥ colon፦ Preface colon (introduces speech from a descriptive prefix)፧ question mark፨ paragraph separator

Grammar

Simple Amharic sentences

One may construct simple Amharic sentences by using a subject and a predicate. Here are a few simple sentences:

ኢትዮጵያ አፍሪቃ ውስጥ ናት፡

Ityoppya ʾAfriqa wəsṭ nat (lit., Ethiopia Africa inside is)'Ethiopia is in Africa.'

ልጁ ተኛቷልLəǧu täññätʷ

all. (lit., the boy is asleep) -u is a definite article. Ləǧ is 'boy'. Ləǧu is 'the boy"The boy is asleep.'

አየሩ ደስ ይ

ሏAyyäru däss yəlall. (lit., the weather pleasant is)'The weather is pleasant.'

እሱ ወደ ከተማ መጣ

Əssu wädä kätäma mäṭṭa. (lit., he to city came)'He came to the city.'

Pronouns

Personal pronouns

In most languages, there are a small number of basic distinctions of person, number, and often gender that play a role within the grammar of the language. We see these distinctions within the basic set of independent personal pronouns, for example, English I, Amharic እኔ әne; English she, Amharic እሷ әsswa. In Amharic, as in other Semitic languages, the same distinctions appear in three other places within the grammar of the languages.

Subject-verb agreement

All Amharic verbs agree with their subjects; that is, the person, number, and (second- and third - person singular) gender of the subject of the verb are marked by suffixes or prefixes on the verb. Because the affixes that signal subject agreement vary greatly with the particular verb tense/aspect/mood, they are normally not considered to be pronouns and are discussed elsewhere in this article under verb conjugation.

Object pronoun suffixes

Amharic verbs often have additional morphology that indicates the person, number, and (second - and third - person singular) gender of the object of the verb.

አልማዝን አየኋት

almazən ayyähʷ-at

Almaz-ACC I-saw-her

'I saw Almaz'

While morphemes such as -at in this example are sometimes described as signaling object agreement, analogous to subject agreement, they are more often thought of as object pronoun suffixes because, unlike the markers of subject agreement, they do not vary significantly with the tense/aspect/mood of the verb. For arguments of the verb other than the subject or the object, there are two separate sets of related suffixes, one with a benefactive meaning (to, for), the other with an adversative or locative meaning (against', to the detriment of, on', at).

ለአልማዝ በሩን ከፈትኩላት

läʾalmaz bärrun käffätku-llat

for-Almaz door-DEF-ACC I-opened-for-her

'I opened the door for Almaz'

በአልማዝ በሩን ዘጋሁባት

bäʾalmaz bärrun zäggahu-bbat

on-Almaz door-DEF-ACC I-closed-on-her

'I closed the door on Almaz (to her detriment)'

Morphemes such as -llat and -bbat in these examples will be referred to in this article as prepositional object pronoun suffixes because they correspond to prepositional phrases such as for her and on her, to distinguish them from the direct object pronoun suffixes such as -at 'her'.

Possessive suffixes

Amharic has a further set of morphemes that are suffixed to nouns, signalling possession: ቤት bet 'house', ቤቴ bete, my house, ቤቷ; betwa, her house.

In each of these four aspects of the grammar, independent pronouns, subject–verb agreement, object pronoun suffixes, and possessive suffixes, Amharic distinguishes eight combinations of person, number, and gender. For first person, there is a two-way distinction between singular (I) and plural (we), whereas for second and third persons, there is a distinction between singular and plural and within the singular a further distinction between masculine and feminine (you m. sg., you f. sg., you pl., he, she, they).

Amharic is a pro-drop language. That is, neutral sentences in which no element is emphasized normally do not have independent pronouns: ኢትዮጵያዊ ነው 'ityoppyawi näw 'he's Ethiopian', ጋበዝኳት gabbäzkwat 'I invited her'. The Amharic words that translate he, I, and her do not appear in these sentences as independent words. However, in such cases, the person, number, and (second- or third-person singular) gender of the subject and object are marked on the verb. When the subject or object in such sentences is emphasized, an independent pronoun is used: እሱ ኢትዮጵያዊ ነው əssu 'ityoppyawi näw 'he's Ethiopian', እኔ ጋበዝኳት əne gabbäzkwat 'I invited her', እሷን ጋበዝኳት əsswan gabbäzkwat 'I invited her'.

The table below shows alternatives for many of the forms. The choice depends on what precedes the form in question, usually whether this is a vowel or a consonant, for example, for the 1st person singular possessive suffix, አገሬ agär-e 'my country', ገላዬ gäla-ye 'my body'.

Avarice ethaiopa ግርኛ Personalized ግርኛ ehtiopia Pronouns

English	Independent	Object pronoun suffixes			Possessive suffixes
		Direct	Prepositional		
			Benefactive	Locative/Adversative	
I	እኔ əne	-(ä/ə)ñ	-(ə)lləñ	-(ə)bbəñ	-(y)e
you (m. sg.)	አንተ antä	-(ə)h	-(ə)lləh	-(ə)bbəh	-(ə)h
you (f. sg.)	አንቺ anči	-(ə)š	-(ə)lləš	-(ə)bbəš	-(ə)š
you (polite)	እርስዎ ərswo	-(ə)wo(t)	-(ə)lləwo(t)	-(ə)bbəwo(t)	-wo
he	እሱ əssu	-(ä)w, -t	-(ə)llät	-(ə)bbät	-(w)u
she	እሷ əsswa	-at	-(ə)llat	-(ə)bbat	-wa
s/he (polite)	እሳቸው əssaččäw	-aččäw	-(ə)llaččäw	-(ə)bbaččäw	-aččäw
we	እኛ əñña	-(ä/ə)n	-(ə)llən	-(ə)bbən	-aččən
you (pl.)	እናንተ ənnantä	-aččəhu	-(ə)llaččəhu	-(ə)bbaččəhu	-aččəhu
they	እነሱ ənnässu	-aččäw	-(ə)llaččäw	-(ə)bbaččäw	-aččäw

Within second- and third-person singular, there are two additional polite independent pronouns, for reference to people toward whom the speaker wishes to show respect. This usage is an example of the so-called T-V distinction that is made in many languages. The polite pronouns in Amharic are እርስዎ ərswo 'you (sg. polite)'. and እሳቸው əssaččäw 's/he (polite)'. Although these forms are singular semantically — they refer to one person — they correspond to third-person plural elsewhere in the grammar, as is common in other T-V systems. For the possessive pronouns, however, the polite 2nd person has the special suffix -wo 'your sg. pol.'

For possessive pronouns (mine, yours, etc.), Amharic adds the independent pronouns to the preposition yä- 'of': የኔ yäne 'mine', ያንተ yantä 'yours m. sg.', ያንቺ yanči 'yours f. sg.', የሷ yässwa 'hers', etc.

Reflexive pronouns

For reflexive pronouns ('myself', 'yourself', etc.), Amharic adds the possessive suffixes to the noun ራስ ras 'head': ራሴ rase 'myself', ራሷ raswa 'herself', etc.

Demonstrative pronouns

Like English, Amharic makes a two-way distinction between near ('this, these') and far ('that, those') demonstrative expressions (pronouns, adjectives, adverbs). Besides number, as in English, Amharic also distinguishes masculine and feminine gender in the singular.

Amharic Demonstrative Pronouns

Number, Gender		Near	Far
Singular	Masculine	ይህ yəh(ə)	ያ ya
	Feminine	ይቺ yəčči, ይህች yəhəčč	ያቺ yačči
Plural		እነዚህ ənnäzzih	እነዚያ ənnäzziya

There are also separate demonstratives for formal reference, comparable to the formal personal pronouns: እኒህ əññih 'this, these (formal)' and እኒያ ənniya 'that, those (formal)'.

The singular pronouns have combining forms beginning with zz instead of y when they follow a preposition: ስለዚህ säläzzih 'because of this; therefore', እንደዚያ əndäzziya 'like that'. Note that the plural demonstratives, like the second and third person plural personal pronouns, are formed by adding the plural prefix እን ənnä- to the singular masculine forms.

Nouns

Amharic nouns can be primary or derived. A noun like əgər 'foot, leg' is primary, and a noun like əgr-äñña 'pedestrian' is a derived noun.

Gender

Amharic nouns can have a masculine or feminine gender. There are several ways to express gender. An example is the old suffix -t for femininity. This suffix is no longer productive and is limited to certain patterns and some isolated nouns. Nouns and adjectives ending in -awi usually take the suffix -t to form the feminine form, e.g. ityoppya-(a)wi 'Ethiopian (m.)' vs. ityoppya-wi-t 'Ethiopian (f.)'; sämay-awi 'heavenly (m.)' vs. sämay-awi-t 'heavenly (f.)'. This suffix also occurs in nouns and adjective based on the pattern qət(t)ul, e.g. nəgus 'king' vs. nəgəs-t 'queen' and qəddus 'holy (m.)' vs. qəddəs-t 'holy (f.)'.

Some nouns and adjectives take a feminine marker -it: ləğ 'child, boy' vs. ləğ-it 'girl'; bäg 'sheep, ram' vs. bäg-it 'ewe'; šəmagəlle 'senior, elder (m.)' vs. šəmagəll-it 'old woman'; t'ot'a 'monkey' vs. t'ot'-it 'monkey (f.)'. Some nouns have this feminine marker without having a masculine opposite, e.g.

šärär-it 'spider', azur-it 'whirlpool, eddy'. There are, however, also nouns having this -it suffix that are treated as masculine: säraw-it 'army', nägar-it 'big drum'.

The feminine gender is not only used to indicate biological gender, but may also be used to express smallness, e.g. bet-it-u 'the little house' (lit. house-FEM-DEF). The feminine marker can also serve to express tenderness or sympathy.

Specifiers

Amharic has special words that can be used to indicate the gender of people and animals. For people, wänd is used for masculinity and set for femininity, e.g. wänd ləǧ 'boy', set ləǧ 'girl'; wänd hakim 'physician, doctor (m.)', set hakim 'physician, doctor (f.)'. For animals, the words täbat, awra, or wänd (less usual) can be used to indicate masculine gender, and anəst or set to indicate feminine gender. Examples: täbat t'əǧa 'calf (m.)'; awra doro 'cock (rooster)'; set doro 'hen'.

Plural

The plural suffix -očč is used to express plurality of nouns. Some morphophonological alternations occur depending on the final consonant or vowel. For nouns ending in a consonant, plain -očč is used: bet 'house' becomes bet-očč 'houses'. For nouns ending in a back vowel (-a, -o, -u), the suffix takes the form -ʷočč, e.g. wəšša 'dog', wəšša-ʷočč 'dogs'; käbäro 'drum', käbäro-ʷočč 'drums'. Nouns that end in a front vowel pluralize using -ʷočč or -yočč, e.g. ṣähafi 'scholar', ṣähafi-ʷočč or ṣähafi-yočč 'scholars'. Another possibility for nouns ending in a vowel is to delete the vowel and use plain očč, as in wəšš-očč 'dogs'.

Besides using the normal external plural (-očč), nouns and adjectives can be pluralized by way of reduplicating one of the radicals. For example, wäyzäro 'lady' can take the normal plural, yielding wäyzär-očč, but wäyzazər 'ladies' is also found (Leslau 1995:173).

Some kinship-terms have two plural forms with a slightly different meaning. For example, wändəmm 'brother' can be pluralized as wändəmm-očč 'brothers' but also as wändəmmam-ač 'brothers of each other'. Likewise, əhət 'sister' can be pluralized as əhət-očč ('sisters'), but also as ətəmm-am-ač 'sisters of each other'.

In compound words, the plural marker is suffixed to the second noun: betä krəstiyan 'church' (lit. house of Christian) becomes betä krəstiyan-očč 'churches'.

Archaic forms

Amsalu Aklilu has pointed out that Amharic has inherited a large number of old plural forms directly from Classical Ethiopic (Ge'ez) (Leslau 1995:172). There are basically two archaic pluralizing strategies, called external and internal plural. The external plural consists of adding the suffix -an (usually masculine) or -at (usually feminine) to the singular form. The internal plural employs vowel quality or apophony to pluralize words, similar to English man vs. men and goose vs. geese. Sometimes combinations of the two systems are found. The archaic plural forms are sometimes used to form new plurals, but this is only considered grammatical in more established cases.

Examples of the external plural: mämhər 'teacher', mämhər-an; t'äbib 'wise person', t'äbib-an; kahən 'priest', kahən-at; qal 'word', qal-at.

Examples of the internal plural: dəngəl 'virgin', dänagəl; hagär 'land', ahəgur.

Examples of combined systems: nəgus 'king', nägäs-t; kokäb 'star', käwakəb-t; mäs'əhaf 'book', mäs'ahəf-t.

Definiteness

If a noun is definite or specified, this is expressed by a suffix, the article, which is -u or -w for masculine singular nouns and -wa, -itwa or -ätwa for feminine singular nouns. For example:

masculine sg	masculine sg definite	feminine sg	feminine sg definite
bet	bet-u	gäräd	gärad-wa
house	the house	maid	the maid

In singular forms, this article distinguishes between the male and female gender; in plural forms this distinction is absent, and all definites are marked with -u, e.g. bet-očč-u 'houses', gäräd-očč-u 'maids'. As in the plural, morphophonological alternations occur depending on the final consonant or vowel.

Accusative

Amharic has an accusative marker, -(ə)n. Its use is related to the definiteness of the object, thus Amharic shows differential object marking. In general, if the object is definite, possessed, or a proper noun, the accusative must be used (Leslau 1995: pp. 181 ff.).

ləǧ-u	wəšša-w-ən	abbarär-ä.
child-def	dog-def-acc	chase-3msSUBJ
'The child chased the dog.'		
*ləǧ-u	wəšša-w	abbarär-ä.
child-def	dog-def	chase-3msSUBJ
'The child chased the dog.'		

The accusative suffix is usually placed after the first word of the noun phrase:

Yəh-ən	sä'at	gäzz-ä.
this-acc	watch	buy-3msSUBJ

'He bought this watch.'

Nominalization

Amharic has various ways to derive nouns from other words or other nouns. One way of nominalizing consists of a form of vowel agreement (similar vowels on similar places) inside the three-radical structures typical of Semitic languages. For example:

CəCäC: — ṭəbäb 'wisdom'; həmäm 'sickness'

CəCCaC-e: — wəffar-e 'obesity'; č'əkkan-e 'cruelty'

CəC-ät: — rəṭb-ät 'moistness'; 'əwq-ät 'knowledge'; wəfr-ät 'fatness'.

There are also several nominalizing suffixes.

-ənna: — 'relation'; krəst-ənna 'Christianity'; sənf-ənna 'laziness'; qes-ənna 'priesthood'.

-e, suffixed to place name X, yields 'a person from X': goğğam-e 'someone from Gojjam'.

-äñña and -täñña serve to express profession, or some relationship with the base noun: əgr-äñña 'pedestrian' (from əgər 'foot'); bärr-äñña 'gate-keeper' (from bärr 'gate').

-ənnät and -nnät — '-ness'; ityoppyawi-nnät 'Ethiopianness'; qərb-ənnät 'nearness' (from qərb 'near').

Verbs

Conjugation

As in other Semitic languages, Amharic verbs use a combination of prefixes and suffixes to indicate the subject, distinguishing 3 persons, two numbers and (in all persons except first-person and "honorific" pronouns) two genders.

Gerund

Along with the infinitive and the present participle, the gerund is one of three non-finite verb forms. The infinitive is a nominalized verb, the present participle expresses incomplete action, and the gerund expresses completed action, e.g. ali məsa bälto wädä gäbäya hedä 'Ali, having eaten lunch, went to the market'. There are several usages of the gerund depending on its morpho-syntactic features.

Verbal use

The gerund functions as the head of a subordinate clause (see the example above). There may be more than one gerund in one sentence. The gerund is used to form the following tense forms:

የእንግሊዝኛ / አማርኛ የአነጋገር መዝገበ ቃላት   77

present perfect nägro -all/näbbär 'He has said'.

past perfect nägro näbbär 'He had said'.

possible perfect nägro yəhonall 'He (probably) has said'.

Adverbial use

The gerund can be used as an adverb: alfo alfo yəsəqall 'Sometimes he laughs'. (From ማለፍ 'to pass'; lit. "passing passing") əne dägmo mämṭat əfälləgallähu 'I also want to come'. (From መድገም 'to repeat'; lit. "I, repeating, want to come")

Adjectives

Adjectives are words or constructions used to qualify nouns. Adjectives in Amharic can be formed in several ways: they can be based on nominal patterns, or derived from nouns, verbs and other parts of speech. Adjectives can be nominalized by way of suffixing the nominal article (see Nouns above). Amharic has few primary adjectives. Some examples are dägg 'kind, generous', dəda 'mute, dumb, silent', bičа 'yellow'.

Nominal patterns

CäCCaC — käbbad 'heavy'; läggas 'generous'CäC(C)iC — räqiq 'fine, subtle'; addis 'new'CäC(C)aCa — säbara 'broken'; ṭämama 'bent, wrinkled'CəC(C)əC — bələh 'intelligent, smart';

dəbbəq' 'hidden'CəC(C)uC — kəbur 'worthy, dignified'; t'əqur 'black'; qəddus 'holy'

Denominalizing suffixes

-äñña — hayl-äñña 'powerful' (from hayl 'power'); əwnät-äñña 'true' (from əwnät 'truth')-täñña — aläm-täñña 'secular' (from aläm 'world')-awi — ləbb-awi 'intelligent' (from ləbb 'heart'); mədr-awi 'earthly' (from mədr 'earth'); haymanot-awi 'religious' (from haymanot 'religion')

Prefix yə

yə-kätäma 'urban' (lit. 'from the city'); yə-krästänna 'Christian' (lit. 'of Christianity'); yə-wəšhet 'wrong' (lit. 'of falsehood').

Adjective noun complex

The adjective and the noun together are called the 'adjective noun complex'. In Amharic, the adjective precedes the noun, with the verb last; e.g. kəfu geta 'a bad master'; təlləq bet särra (lit. big house he-built) 'he built a big house'.

If the adjective noun complex is definite, the definite article is suffixed to the adjective and not to the noun, e.g. təlləq-u bet (lit. big-def house) 'the big house'. In a possessive construction, the adjective takes the definite article, and the noun takes the pronominal possessive suffix, e.g. təlləq-u bet-e (lit. big-def house-my) "my big house".

When enumerating adjectives using -nna 'and', both adjectives take the definite article: qonğo-wa-nna astäway-wa ləğ mäṭṭačč (lit. pretty-def-and intelligent-def girl came) "the pretty and intelligent girl came". In the case of an indefinite plural adjective noun complex, the noun is plural and the adjective may be used in singular or in plural form. Thus, 'diligent students' can be rendered təgu tämari^wočč (lit. diligent student-PLUR) or təgu^wočč tämari^wočč (lit. diligent-PLUR student-PLUR).

Dialects

There has not been much published about Amharic dialect differences. All dialects are mutually intelligible, but certain minor variations are noted.[15][16]

Mittwoch described a form of Amharic spoken by the descendants of Weyto language speakers,[17] but it was likely not a dialect of Amharic so much as the result of incomplete language learning as the community shifted languages from Weyto to Amharic.

Conversation

ንግግር   nigigiri

Do you speak (English/ Amharic)? አማርኛ ትናገራለህ? [ʾämarəña tənagäralähə?]

Just a little በመጠኑ [bämätʾänu]

I like Amharic አማርኛን እወዳለሁ [ʾämarəñanə ʾəwädalähu]

Can I practice with you? ከአንተ ጋር መለማመድ እችላለሁ? [käʾänətä garə mälämamädə ʾəčəlalähu?]

How old are you? ስንት ዓመትህ ነው? [sənətə ʾamätəhə näwə?]

I'm thirty three years old ሰላሳ ሶስት ዓመቴ ነው [sälasa sosətə ʾamäte näwə]

It was nice talking to you ከአንተ ጋር በማውራቴ ደስ ብሎኛል [käʾänətä garə bämawərate däsə bəloñalə]

hi ሃይ [hayə]

How are you? እንዴት ነህ? [ʾənədetə nähə?]

I'm good, thank you ደህና ነኝ, አመሰግናለው [dähəna näñə, ʾämäsägənaläwə]

and you? አንተስ? [ʾänətäsə?]

What is your name? ስምህ ማነው? [səməhə manäwə?]

My name is Maya ማያ [maya]

Nice to meet you አንተን በማግኘቴ ደስ ብሎኛል [ʼänətänə bämagəñäte däsə bəloñalə]

I have a reservation (hotel) ቀደም ብዬ ይዣለሁ [qädämə bəye yəžalähu]

Do you have rooms available? መኝታ ክፍሎች ይኖራችኋል? [mäñəta kəfəločə yənoračəhalə?]

I would like a non-smoking room ሲጋራ የማይጨስበት ክፍል አፈልጋለሁ [sigara yämayəč'äsəbätə kəfələ ʾəfäləgalähu]

What is the charge per night? ለአዳር ስንት ይከፈላል? [läʾädarə sənətə yəkəfälalə?]

Is this seat taken? ሰው አለው? [säwə ʾäläwə?]

I'm vegetarian አትክልት ተመጋቢ ነኝ [ʾätəkələtə tämägabi näñə]

Waiter አስተናጋጅ [ʾäsətänagağə]

How much is this? ስንት ነው? [sənətə näwə?]

This is very expensive በጣም ውድ ነው [bät'amə wədə näwə]

Animals

እንስሳት inisisati

Bird	ወፍ	wefi
Butterfly	ቢራቢሮ	bīrabīro
Cat	ድመት	dimeti
Cow	ላም	lami
Dog	ውሻ	wisha
Donkey	አህያ	āhiya
Duck	ዳክዬ	dakiye
Eagle	ንሥር	neširi
Elephant	ዝሆን	zihoni
Frog	እንቁራሪት	ānik'urarīti
Goose	ዝዬ	ziyī
Gorilla	ገመሬ	gemerē
Horse	ፈረስ	feresi
Lion	አንበሳ	ānibesa
Monkey	ዝንጀሮ	zinijero
Mouse	አይጥ	āyit'i
Parrot	በቅቢቃ	bek'ibek'a

Pig	አሳማ	āsama
Scorpion	ጊንጥ	gīnit'i
Sheep	በግ	begi
Snake	እባብ	ibabi
Turtle	ኤሊ	ēlī
Zebra	የሜዳ አህያ	yemēda āhiya

Transportation

መጓጓዣ megwagwazha

bicycle	ቢስክሌት	bīsikilēti
boat	ጀልባ	jeliba
bus	አውቶቡስ	āwitobusi
car	መኪና	mekīna
drive	ድራይቭ	dirayivi
gasoline	ቤንዚን	bēnizīni
road	መንገድ	menigedi
ship	መርከብ	merikebi
sign	ምልክት	milikiti
stop	ተወ	tewe
tire	ጎማ	goma
train	ባቡር	baburi
Truck	ትራክ	tiraki

Directions

አቅጣጫዎች   āk'it'ach'awochi

bottom	ታች	tachi
down	ወደታች	wedetachi
east	ምስራቅ	misirak'i
far	ሩቅ	ruk'i
left	ግራ	gira
low	ዝቅ ያለ	zik'i yale
near	ቅርብ	k'iribi
north	ሰሜን	semēni
right	ቀኝ	k'enyi
side	ወገን	wegeni
south	ደቡብ	debubi
up	እስከ	isike
west	ምዕራብ	mi'irabi

Places

ቦታዎች botawochi

beach	የባሕር ዳርቻ	yebahiri daricha
church	ቤተ ክርስቲያን	bēte kirisitiyani
city	ከተማ	ketema
country	አገር	āgeri
farm	እርሻ	irisha
hotel	ሆቴል	hotēli
library	ቤተ መጻሕፍት	bēte mets'ahifiti
location	አካባቢ	ākababī
map	ካርታ	karita
market	ገበያ	gebeya
office	ቢሮ	bīro
park	መናፈሻ	menafesha
prison	እስር ቤት	isiri bēti
restaurant	ምግብ ቤት	migibi bēti
school	ትምህርት ቤት	timihiriti bēti
station	መሳፈሪያ	mešaferīya
street	መንገድ	menigedi
theater	ትያትር ቤት	tiyatiri bēti
town	ከተማ	ketema
university	ዩኒቨርሲቲ	yunīverisītī

Clothing

ልብስ   libisi

belt	ቀበቶ	k'ebeto
blouse	የሴቶች ሸሚዝ	yesētochi shemīzi
boot	ቦት ጫማ	boti ch'ama
cap	ቆብ	k'obi
clothing	ልብስ	libisi
coat	ካፖርት	kaporiti
dress	ልብስ	libisi
gloves	ጓንት	gwaniti
hat	ባርኔጣ	barinēt'a
jacket	ጉርድ ኮት	guridi koti
jeans	ጂንስ	jīnisi
pants	ሱሪ	surī
shirt	ሸሚዝ	shemīzi
shoe	ጫማ	ch'ama
skirt	ጉርድ ቀሚስ	guridi k'emīsi
suit	ሙሉ ልብስ	mulu libisi
T-shirt	ቲ-ቲሸርት	tī - tīsheriti
wear	መልበስ	melibesi

Colors

ቀለማት   k'elemati

black	ጥቁር	t'ik'uri
blue	ሰማያዊ	semayawī
brown	ብናማ	binama
clear	ግልጽ	gilits'i
color	ቀለም	k'elemi
cream	ቅባት	k'ibati
dark	ጥቁር	t'ik'uri
gray	ግራጫ	girach'a
green	አረንጓዴ	ārenigwadē
pink	ብሩህ ቀይ	biruhi k'eyi
red	ቀይ	k'eyi
white	ነጭ	nech'i

My house is white.

[noun + adjective] ቤቴ ነጭ ነው [bete näč'ə näwə]

I have a small green house

[adjective + adjective] ትንሽ አረንጓዴ ቤት አለኝ [tənəšə ˀäränəgäde betə ˀäläñə]

የእንግሊዝኛ / አማርኛ የእነጋር መዝገብ ቃላት

People

ሕዝብ hizibi

adult	አዋቂ	āwak'ī
boy	ወንድ ልጅ	wenidi liji
child	ሕፃን	hits'ani
king	ንጉሥ	niguši
neighbor	ጎረቤት	gorebēti
people	ሕዝብ	hizibi
priest	ቄስ	k'ēsi
queen	ንግሥት	nigišiti

Jobs

ሥራዎች sirawochi

Baker	ዳቦ ጋጋሪ	dabo gagarī
Dancer	ደናሽ	denashi
Job	ሥራ	šira
Lawyer	ነገረፈጅ	negerefeji
Police	ፖሊስ	polīsi
President	ፕሬዚዳንት	pirēzīdaniti
Reporter	ጋዜጠኛ	gazēt'enya
Secretary	ጸሐፊ	ts'eḫāfī
Soldier	ወታደር	wetaderi
Student	ተማሪ	temarī
Waiter	አሳላፊ	āsalafī
Work	ሥራ	šira

Society

ማኅበር mahiberi

Ballot	የምርጫ ወረቀት	yemirich'a werek'eti
Democracy	ዴሞክራሲ	dēmokirasī
Election	ምርጫ	mirich'a
Mayor	ከንቲባ	kenitība
Play	ይጫወታሉ	yich'awetalu
Vote	ድምጽ	dimits'i
War	ጦርነት	t'orineti

Art

ሥነ ጥበብ   šine t'ibebi

abstract	ረቂቅ	rek'īk'i
art	ሥነ ጥበብ	šine t'ibebi
artist	ሠዓሊ	še'alī
easel	መያዣ	meyazha
gallery	የሥዕል ማሳያ አዳራሽ	yeši'ili masaya ādarashi
master	ባለቤት	balebēti
portrait	የቁም	yek'umi

Beverages

መጠጦች   met'et'ochi

alcohol	አልኮል	ālikoli
beer	ቢራ	bīra
coffee	ቡና	buna
drink	ጠጣ	t'et'a
juice	ጭማቂ	ch'imak'ī
tea	ሻይ	shayi
water	ውሃ	wiha
Whiskey	ውስኪ	wisikī
Wine	የወይን ጠጅ	yeweyini t'eji

English / Amharic Dictionary

Food

ምግብ migibi

apple	ፖም	pami
banana	ሙዝ	muzi
beef	የበሬ ሥጋ	yeberē šiga
bread	ዳቦ	dabo
breakfast	ቁርስ	k'urisi
butter	ቅቤ	k'ibē
cake	ኬክ	kēki
cheese	የደረቀ አይብ	yederek'e āyibi
chicken	ጫጩት	ch'ach'īti
corn	በቆሎ	bek'olo
dinner	እራት	irati
eat	መብላት	mebilati
egg	እንቁላል	inik'ulali
fish	ዓሣ	'aša
food	ምግብ	migibi
fork	ሹካ	vuka
ice	በረዶ	beredo
knife	ቢላዋ	bīlawa
lemon	ሎሚ	lomī
lunch	ምሳ	misa
milk	ወተት	weteti
orange	ብርቱካናማ	biritukanama
plate	ሳህን	šahini
pork	ያሣማ ሥጋ	yašama šiga
rice	ሩዝ	ruzi

salt	ጨው	ch'ewi
silver	ብር	biri
soup	ሾርባ	shoriba
spoon	ማንካ	manika

Do you have milk?

[verb + noun] ወተት አለህ? [wätätə ʾälähə?]

I have milk and coffee

[preposition + noun] ወተት እና ቡና አለኝ [wätätə ʾəna buna ʾäläñə]

He has three apples.

[number + plural noun] ሶስት ፖሞች አለው [sosətə pomočə ʾäläwə]

She only has one apple. [number + singular noun] አንድ ፖም ብቻ ነው ያላት [ʾänədə pomə bəča näwə yalatə]

We live in a small house.

[adjective + noun] ትንሽ ቤት ውስጥ እንኖራለን [tənəšə betə wəsət'ə ʾənənoralänə]

I like our breakfast.

[pronoun + noun] ቁርሳችንን ወድጀዋለው [qurəsačənənə wädəǧewaläwə]

Home

መኖሪያ ቤት menorīya bēti

Bedroom	መኝታ ቤት	menyita bēti
Ceiling	ጣሪ	t'ara
Chair	ወምበር	wemiberi
Door	በር	beri
Garden	የአትክልት	ye'ātikiliti
Home	መኖሪያ ቤት	menorīya bēti
House	ቤት	bēti
Inside	ውስጥ	wisit'i
Key	ቁልፍ	k'ulifi
Kitchen	ወጥ ቤት	wet'i bēti
Lamp	ሙብራት	mebirati
Lock	ቁልፍ	k'ulifi
Outside	ውጭ	wich'i
Roof	ጣሪ	t'ara
Room	ክፍል	kifili
Table	ጠረጴዛ	t'erep'ēza
Toilet	ሽንት ቤት	shiniti bēti
Window	መስኮት	mesikoti
Yard	ያርድ	yaridi

የእንግሊዝኛ / አማርኛ የእነጋገር መዝገበ ቃላት 99

Electronics

ኤሌክትሮኒክስ   ēlēkitironīkisi

camera	ካሜራ	kamēra
computer	ኮምፒዩተር	komipiyuteri
electronics	ኤሌክትሮኒክስ	ēlēkitironīkisi
laptop	ላፕቶፕ	lapitopi
phone	ስልክ	siliki
radio	ራዲዮን	radīyoni
snow	በረዶ	beredo
telephone	ስልክ	siliki
television	ቴሌቪዥን	tēlēvīzhini

Nature

ፍጥረት fit'ireti

dry	ደረቅ	derek'i
earth	መሬት	merēti
forest	ደን	deni
ground	መሬት	merēti
hill	ኮረብታ	korebita
hot	ሙቅ	muk'i
island	ደሴት	desēti
lake	ሐይቅ	hāyik'i
leaf	ቅጠል	k'it'eli
moon	ጨረቃ	ch'erek'a
mountain	ተራራ	terara
nature	ፍጥረት	fit'ireti
ocean	ውቅያኖስ	wik'iyanosi
plant	ተክል	tekili
pool	መዋኛ	mewanya
river	ወንዝ	wenizi
root	ሥር	širi
sand	አሸዋ	āshewa
sea	ባሕር	bahiri
seed	ዘር	zeri
sky	ሰማይ	semayi
soil	አፈር	āferi

የእንግሊዝኛ / አማርኛ የእነጋር መዝገብ ቃላት   101

space	ቦታ	bota
star	ኮከብ	kokebi
stone	ድንጋይ	dinigayi
sun	ጸሐይ	ts'ehāyi
tree	ዛፍ	zafi
valley	ሸለቆ	shelek'o
wave	ማዕበል	ma'ibeli
world	ዓለም	'alemi

Measurements

መመጠን memet'eni

centimeter	ሳንቲሜትር	sanitīmētiri
inch	ኢንች	īnichi
kilogram	ግራም	girami
Measurement	መመጠን	memet'eni
Meter	መቀጠሪያ	mek'ut'erīya
Pound	ፓው.ንድ	pawunidi
Square	አራት ማዕዘን	ārati ma'izeni
Temperature	ትኩሳት	tikusati
Weight	ሚዛን	mīzani

Directions

አቅጣጫዎች āk'it'ach'awochi

bottom	ታች	tachi
down	ወደታች	wedetachi
east	ምስራቅ	misirak'i
far	ሩቅ	ruk'i
left	ግራ	gira
low	ዝቅ ያለ	zik'i yale
near	ቅርብ	k'iribi
north	ሰሜን	semēni
right	ቀኝ	k'enyi
side	ወገን	wegeni
south	ደቡብ	debubi
up	እስከ	isike
west	ምዕራብ	mi'irabi

Seasons

ወቅት wek'iti

Autumn	በልግ	beligi
Spring	ምንጋው	minich'i
summer	በጋ	bega
Winter	ክረምት	kiremiti

Numbers

ቁጥሮች   k'ut'irochi

zero	ዜሮ	zēro
one	አንድ	ānidi
two	ሁለት	huleti
three	ሶስት	sositi
four	አራት	ārati
five	አምስት	āmisiti
six	ስድስት	sidisiti
seven	ሰባት	sebati
eight	ስምት	simiti
nine	ዘጠኝ	zet'enyi
ten	አስር	āsiri
eleven	አስራ አንድ	āsira ānidi
twelve	አስራ ሁለት	āsira huleti
thirteen	አስራ ሶስት	āsira sositi
fourteen	አስራ አራት	āsira ārati
fifteen	አስራ አምስት	āsira āmisiti
sixteen	አስራ ስድስት	āsira sidisiti
seventeen	አስራ ሰባት	āsira sebati
eighteen	አስራ ስምንት	āsira siminiti
nineteen	አስራ ዘጠኝ	āsira zet'enyi
twenty	ሃያ	haya
twenty-one	ሃያ አንድ	haya ānidi
twenty-two	ሃያ ሁለት	haya huleti
twenty-three	ሃያ ሶስት	haya sositi

twenty-four	ሃያ አራት	haya ārati
twenty-five	ሃያ አምስት	haya āmisiti
twenty-six	ሃያ ስድስት	haya sidisiti
twenty-seven	ሃያ ሰባት	haya sebati
twenty-eight	ሃያ-ስምንት	haya - siminiti
twenty-nine	ሃያ ዘጠኝ	haya zet'enyi
thirty	ሰላሳ	selasa
forty	አርባ	āriba
fifty	ሃምሳ	hamisa
sixty	ስልሳ	silisa
seventy	ሰባ	seba
eighty	ሰማንያ	semaniya
ninety	ዘጠና	zet'ena
one hundred	አንድ መቶ	ānidi meto
one thousand	አንድ ሺህ	ānidi shīhi
one thousand and one	አንድ ሺህ አንድ	ānidi shīhi ānidi

Months

ወሮች werochi

January	ጥር	t'iri
February	የካቲት	yekatīti
March	መጋቢት	megabīti
April	ሚያዚያ	mīyazīya
May	ግንቦት	giniboti
June	ሰኔ	senē
July	ሐምሌ	hāmilē
August	ነሐሴ	nehāsē
September	መስከረም	mesikeremi
October	ጥቅምት	t'ik'imiti
November	ህዳር	hidari
December	ታህሳስ	tahisasi

Days

ቀናት k'enati

Sunday	እሁድ	ihudi
Monday	ሰኞ	senyo
Tuesday	ማክሰኞ	makisenyo
Wednesday	እሮብ	irobi
Thursday	ሐሙስ	ḥāmusi
Friday	እርብ	āribi
Saturday	ቅዳሜ	k'idamē

Time

ጊዜ gīzē

Afternoon	ከሰአት	kese'āti
Clock	ሰዓት	se'ati
Evening	ምሽት	mishiti
Hour	ሰአት	se'āti
Minute	ደቂቃ	dek'īk'a
Morning	ጠዋት	t'ewati
Night	ሌሊት	lelīti
Today	ዛሬ	zarē
Tomorrow	ነገ	nege
Year	አመት	āmeti
Yesterday	ትናንትና	tinanitina

Body

አካል ākali

arm	ክንድ	kinidi
bone	አጥንት	āt'initi
brain	አአምሮ	ā'imiro
cheeks	ጉንጯቹ	gunich'ochu
chest	ትልቅ ሣጥን	tilik'i šat'ini
chin	አገጪ	āgech'i
elbow	ክንድ	kinidi
eye	ዓይን	'ayini
face	ፊት	fīti
fingers	ጣቶች	t'atochi
foot	እግር	igiri
hair	ጠጉር	t'eguri
hand	እጅ	iji
head	ራስ	rasi
heart	ልብ	libi
knee	ጉልበት	gulibeti
leg	እግር	igiri
neck	አንገት	ānigeti
nose	አፍንጫ	āfinich'a
shoulder	ትክሻ	tikesha
skin	ቆዳ	k'oda
stomach	ሆድ	hodi
sweat	ላብ	labi
teeth	ጥርስ	t'irisi

thigh	ጭን	ch'ini
throat	ጉሮሮ	guroro
thumb	አዉራ ጣት	āwura t'ati
toe	የእግር ጣት	ye'igiri t'ati
Tooth	ጥርስ	t'irisi

English / Amharic Dictionary

Medical

የሕክምና yeḥikimina

blind	ዕውር	'iwiri
blood	ደም	demi
dead	የሞተ	yemote
deaf	ደንቆሮ	denik'oro
drug	መድሃኒት	medihanīti
ear	ጆሮ	joro
healthy	ጤናማ	t'ēnama
hospital	ሐኪም ቤት	ḥākīmi bēti
injury	ጉዳት	gudati
kill	መግደል	megideli
medicine	መድሃኒት	medihanīti
pain	ሕመም	ḥimemi
patient	ትዕግሥተኛ	ti'igišitenya
poison	መርዝ	merizi
sick	የታመመ	yetameme

Money

ገንዘብ genizebi

bank	ባንክ	Baniki
cheap	ርካሽ	Rikashi
dollar	ዶላር	Dolari
money	ገንዘብ	genizebi
price	ዋጋ	Waga
sell	መሸጥ	meshet'i
store	መደብር	medebiri

Family

ቤተሰብ bētesebi

brother	ወንድም	wenidimi
child	ሕፃን	hits'ani
daughter	ሴት ልጅ	sēti liji
father	አባት	ābati
female	ሴት	sēti
girl	ሴት ልጅ	sēti liji
grandfather	ወንድ አያት	wenidi āyati
grandmother	ሴት አያት	sēti āyati
husband	ባል	bali
male	ተባዕት	teba'iti
man	ሰው	sewi
marriage	ጋብቻ	gabicha
marry	ማግባት	magibati
mother	እናት	inati
parent	ወላጅ	welaji
relationship	ግንኙነት	gininyuneti
sister	እህት	ihiti
son	ወንድ ልጅ	wenidi liji
wedding	ሰርግ	serigi
wife	ሚስት	mīsiti
woman	ሴት	sēti

My son is a student.

[masculine + noun] ወንድ ልጅ ተማሪ ነው [wänədə ləğe tämari näwə]

Her daughter is a student.

[feminine + noun] ሴት ልጇዋ ተማሪ ነች [setə ləǧəwa tämari näčə]

He has a tall brother.

[adjective + masculine] ረጅም ወንድም አለው [räǧəmə wänədəmə ʾäläwə]

She has a tall sister

[adjective + feminine] ረጅም እህት አላት [räǧəmə ʾəhətə ʾälatə]

His brothers are young.

[plural masculine + adjective] ወንድሞቹ ወጣቶች ናቸው [wänədəmoču wätʼatočə načäwə]

His sisters are young.

[plural feminine + adjective] እህቶቹ ወጣቶች ናቸው [ʾəhətoču wätʼatočə načäwə]

English / Amharic/ Transliteration

abstract	ረቂቅ	rek'īk'i
actor	የቴአትር ተጫዋች	yetē'ātiri tech'awachi
actress	የቴአትር ተጫዋች	yetē'ātiri tech'awachi
adjectives	ቅጽሎችን	k'its'ilochini
adult	አዋቂ	āwak'ī
afternoon	ከሰአት	kese'āti
air	አየር	āyeri
airport	የአውሮፕላን ማረፊያ	ye'āwiropilani marefīya
alcohol	አልኮል	ālikoli
alcoholic drink	የአልኮል መጠጥ	ye'ālikoli met'et'i
alive	በሕይወት	behiyiweti
Animals	እንስሳት	inisisati
apartment	መኖሪያ ቤት	menorīya bēti
apple	ፖም	pami
April	ሚያዚያ	mīyazīya
architect	አርኪቴክት	ārikītēkiti
arm	ክንድ	kinidi
army	ጦር ሠራዊት	t'ori šerawīti
art	ሥነ ጥበብ	šine t'ibebi
artist	ሠዓሊ	še'alī
attack	ጥቃት	t'ik'ati
August	ነሐሴ	nehāsē
author	ደራሲ	derasī
autumn	በልግ	**beligi**
baby	ሕፃን ልጅ	hits'ani liji
back	ወደኋላ	wedehwala

back	ወደኋላ	wedeḫwala
bad	መጥፎ	met'ifo
bag	ቦርሳ	borisa
baker	ዳቦ ጋጋሪ	dabo gagarī
ball	ኳስ	kwasi
ballot	የምርጫ ወረቀት	yemirich'a werek'eti
banana	ሙዝ	muzi
band	ጓድ	gwadi
bank	ባንክ	baniki
bar	ቡና ቤት	buna bēti
bathroom	መጣጠቢያ ክፍል	met'at'ebīya kifili
beach	የባህር ዳርቻ	yebahiri daricha
beard	ጢም	t'īmi
beat	መምታት	memitati
beautiful	ቆንጆ	k'onijo
bed	አልጋ	āliga
bedroom	መኛታ ቤት	menyita bēti
beef	የበሬ ሥጋ	yeberē šiga
beer	ቢራ	bīra
belt	ቀበቶ	k'ebeto
bend	ጎበጠ	gobet'e
bicycle	ቢስክሌት	bīsikilēti
big	ትልቅ	tilik'i
bill	ሂሳቡ	hīsabu
billion	ቢሊዮን	bīlīyoni
bird	ወፍ	wefi
black	ጥቁር	t'ik'uri
blind	ዕውር	'iwiri
blood	ደም	demi

English / Amharic Dictionary

blouse	የሴቶች ሸሚዝ	yesētochi shemīzi
blue	ሰማያዊ	semayawī
boat	ጀልባ	jeliba
body	አካል	ākali
bone	አጥንት	āt'initi
book	መጽሐፍ	mets'iḫāfi
boot	ቦት ጫማ	boti ch'ama
bottle	ጠርሙዝ	t'erimuzi
bottom	ታች	tachi
box	ሳጥን	sat'ini
boy	ወንድ ልጅ	wenidi liji
brain	አእምሮ	ā'imiro
bread	ዳቦ	dabo
break	እረፍት	irefiti
breakfast	ቁርስ	k'urisi
bridge	ድልድይ	dilidiyi
brother	ወንድም	wenidimi
brown	ብናማ	binama
build	መገንባት	megenibati
building	ሕንጻ	hinits'a
burn	ያቃጥለዋል	yak'at'ilewali
bus	አውቶቡስ	āwitobusi
butter	ቅቤ	k'ibē
butterfly	ቢራቢሮ	bīrabīro
buy	ለመግዛት	lemegizati
buy	ለመግዛት	lemegizati
by	በ	be
cake	ኬክ	kēki
call	ጥሪ	t'irī

camera	ካሜራ	kamēra
camp	ሠፈር	šeferi
candidate	እጩ	ich'u
cap	ቆብ	k'obi
car	መኪና	mekīna
card	ካርድ	karidi
carry	መሸከም	meshekemi
cat	ድመት	dimeti
catch	ያዘ	yaze
ceiling	ጣራ	t'ara
cell	ሕዋስ	ḥiwasi
centimeter	ሳንቲሜትር	sanitīmētiri
chair	ወምበር	wemiberi
cheap	ርካሽ	rikashi
cheeks	ጉንጮቹ	gunich'ochu
cheese	የደረቀ አይብ	yederek'e āyibi
chest	ትልቅ ሣጥን	tilik'i šat'ini
chicken	ጫጩት	ch'ach'īti
child	ሕፃን	hits'ani
child	ሕፃን	hits'ani
chin	አገጭ	āgech'i
church	ቤተ ክርስቲያን	bēte kirisitiyani
circle	ክበብ	kibebi
city	ከተማ	ketema
clay	ሸክላ	shekila
clean	ንጹሕ	nits'uhi
clear	ግልጽ	gilits'i
clock	ሰዓት	se'ati
close	ገጠመ	get'eme
clothing	ልብስ	libisi

club	ዱላ	dila
coat	ካፖርት	kaporiti
coffee	ቡና	buna
cold	ብርድ	biridi
color	ቀለም	k'elemi
computer	ኮምፒዩተር	komipiyuteri
consonant	ድምጽ ተቀባይ ፊደል	dimits'i tek'ebayi fīdeli
contract	ስምምነት	simimineti
cook	ወጥ ቤት ሴት	wet'i bēti sēti
cool	ጥሩ	t'iru
copper	መዳብ	medabi
corn	በቆሎ	bek'olo
corner	ማዕዘን	ma'izeni
count	ተጎዳሁ:	tegodahu:
country	አገር	āgeri
court	ፍርድ ቤት	firidi bēti
cow	ላም	lami
cream	ቅባት	k'ibati
crowd	ሕዝብ	hizibi
cry	ጩኸ	ch'ohe
cup	ሲኒ	sīnī
curved	ጥምዝ	t'imizi
cut	ቆረጠ	k'oret'e
dance	ዳንስ	danisi
dancer	ደናሽ	denashi
dark	ጥቁር	t'ik'uri
dark	ጥቁር	t'ik'uri
date	ቀን	k'eni

daughter	ሴት ልጅ	sēti liji
day	ቀን	k'eni
dead	የሞተ	yemote
deaf	ደንቆሮ	denik'oro
death	ሞት	moti
December	ታህሳስ	tahisasi
deep	ጥልቅ	t'ilik'i
democracy	ዴሞከራሲ	dēmokirasī
diamond	አልማዝ	ālimazi
dictionary	መዝገበ ቃላት	mezigebe k'alati
die	መሞት	memoti
dig	ቆፈረ	k'ofere
dinner	እራት	irati
directions	አቅጣጫዎች	āk'it'ach'awochi ~
dirty	ቆሻሻ	k'ushasha
disease	በሽታ	beshita
doctor	ሐኪም	ḥākīmi
dog	ውሻ	wisha
dollar	ዶላር	dolari
donkey	አህያ	āhiya
door	በር	beri
dot	ነጥብ	net'ibi
down	ወደታች	wedetachi
draw	መሳል	mesali
dream	ሕልም	hilimi
dress	ልብስ	libisi
drink	ጠጣ	t'et'a
drive	ድራይቭ	dirayivi

English / Amharic Dictionary

drug	መድሃኒት	medihanīti
dry	ደረቅ	derek'i
duck	ዳክየ	dakiye
dust	አፈር	āferi
eagle	ንሥር	neširi
ear	ጆሮ	joro
earth	መሬት	merēti
easel	መያዣ	meyazha
east	ምስራቅ	misirak'i
eat	መብላት	mebilati
edge	ጠርዝ	t'erizi
egg	እንቁላል	inik'ulali
eight	ስምት	simiti
eighteen	አስራ ስምንት	āsira siminiti
eighty	ሰማንያ	semaniya
elbow	ክንድ	kinidi
election	ምርጫ	mirich'a
electronics	ኤሌክትሮኒክስ	ēlēkitironīkisi
elephant	ዝሆን	zihoni
eleven	አስራ አንድ	āsira ānidi
energy	ኃይል	hayili
engine	መኪና	mekīna
engine	መኪና	mekīna
evening	ምሽት	mishiti
exercise	መልመጃ	melimeja
expensive	ውድ	widi
explode	አፈላ	āwale
eye	ዓይን	'ayini
face	ፊት	fīti

fall	ወደቀ	wedek'e
family	ቤተሰብ	bētesebi
fan	ፈን	feni
fan	ፈን	feni
far	ሩቅ	ruk'i
farm	እርሻ	irisha
fast	በፍጥነት	befit'ineti
father	አባት	ābati
February	የካቲት	yekatīti
feed	ምግብ	migibi
female	ሴት	sēti
fifteen	አስራ አምስት	āsira āmisiti
fifty	ሃምሳ	hamisa
fight	ትግል	tigili
find	ማግኘት	maginyeti
finger	ጣት	t'ati
fingers	ጣቶች	t'atochi
fire	እሳት	isati
fish	ዓሣ	'aša
five	አምስት	āmisiti
flat	መኖሪያ ቤት	menorīya bēti
floor	ወለል	weleli
flower	አበባ	ābeba
fly	ዝምብ	zimibi
follow	ተከተል	teketeli
food	ምግብ	migibi
food	ምግብ	migibi
foot	እግር	igiri
forest	ደን	deni
fork	ቡካ	vuka

English / Amharic Dictionary

forty	አርባ	āriba
four	አራት	ārati
fourteen	አስራ አራት	āsira ārati
Friday	አርብ	āribi
frog	እንቁራሪት	ānik'urarīti
front	ፊት	fīti
gallery	የሥዕል ማሳያ አዳራሽ	yeši'ili masaya ādarashi
game	ጨዋታ	ch'ewata
garden	የአትክልት	ye'ātikiliti
gasoline	ቤንዚን	bēnizīni
gift	ስጦታ	sit'ota
giraffe	ቀጭኔ	k'ech'inē
girl	ሴት ልጅ	sēti liji
girl	ሴት ልጅ	sēti liji
glass	ብርጭቆ	birich'ik'o
gloves	ጓንት	gwaniti
God	አምላክ	āmilaki
gold	ወርቅ	werik'i
gold	ወርቅ	werik'i
good	ጥሩ	t'iru
good morning	እንደምን አደርክ	inidemini āderiki
goose	ዝይ	ziyī
gorilla	ገመሬ	gemerē
grandfather	ወንድ አያት	wenidi āyati
grandmother	ሴት አያት	sēti āyati
grass	ሣር	šari
gray	ግራጫ	girach'a
green	አረንጓዴ	ārenigwadē
ground	መሬት	merēti

grow	እያደገ	iyadege
gun	ጠበንጃ	t'ebenija
hair	ጠጉር	t'eguri
half	ግማሽ	gimashi
hand	እጅ	iji
hang	ሰቀለ	sek'ele
happy	ደስተኛ	desitenya
hard	ጠንካራ	t'enikara
hat	ባርኔጣ	barinēt'a
he	እርሱ	irisu
head	ራስ	rasi
healthy	ጤናማ	t'ēnama
hear	ሰማ	sema
heart	ልብ	libi
heat	ሙቀት	muk'eti
heaven	መንግሥተ ሰማያት	menigišite semayati
heavy	ከባድ	kebadi
hell	ሲኦል	sī'oli
high	ከፍ ያለ	kefi yale
hill	ኮረብታ	korebita
hole	ቀዳዳ	k'edada
home	መኖሪያ ቤት	menorīya bēti
horse	ፈረስ	feresi
hospital	ሐኪም ቤት	ḥākīmi bēti
hot	ሙቅ	muk'i
hotel	ሆቴል	hotēli
hour	ሰአት	se'āti
house	ቤት	bēti
husband	ባል	bali

English	Amharic	Transliteration
I	እኔ	inē
ice	በረዶ	beredo
iguana	ኢጓና	īgiwana
image	ምስል	misili
inch	ኢንች	īnichi
injury	ጉዳት	gudati
inside	ውስጥ	wisit'i
instrument	መሣሪያ	mešarīya
island	ደሴት	desēti
island	ደሴት	desēti
it	ይህ	yihi
jacket	ጉርድ ኮት	guridi koti
January	ጥር	t'iri
jeans	ጂንስ	jīnisi
Job	ሥራ	šira
job	ሥራ	šira
juice	ጭማቂ	ch'imak'ī
July	ሐምሌ	hāmilē
jump	ዘለለ	zelele
June	ሰኔ	senē
key	ቁልፍ	k'ulifi
kill	መግደል	megideli
kilogram	ግራም	girami
king	ንጉሥ	niguši
kiss	መሳም	mesami
kitchen	ወጥ ቤት	wet'i bēti
knee	ጉልበት	gulibeti
knife	ቢላዋ	bīlawa
lake	ሐይቅ	ḫāyik'i

lamp	መብራት	mebirati
laptop	ላፕቶፕ	lapitopi
laugh	ሳቅ	sak'i
lawyer	ነገረፈጅ	negerefeji
leaf	ቅጠል	k'it'eli
learn	መማር	memari
left	ግራ	gira
leg	እግር	igiri
lemon	ሎሚ	lomī
letter	ደብዳቤ	debidabē
library	ቤተ መጻሕፍት	bēte mets'aḫifiti
lie down	ጋደም ማለት	gademi maleti
lift	አሳንሰር	āsaniseri
light	መብራት	mebirati
lion	አንበሳ	ānibesa
lip	ከንፈር	keniferi
location	አካባቢ	ākababī
lock	ቁልፍ	k'ulifi
long	ረጅም	rejimi
loose	የተፈታ	yetefeta
lose	ያጣሉ	yat'alu
loud	በታላቅ	betalak'i
love	ፍቅር	fik'iri
low	ዝቅ ያለ	zik'i yale
lunch	ምሳ	misa
magazine	መጽሔት	mets'ihēti
male	ተባዕት	teba'iti
man	ሰው	sewi
manager	አስተዳዳሪ	āsitedadarī
map	ካርታ	karita

March	መጋቢት	megabīti
market	ገበያ	gebeya
marriage	ጋብቻ	gabicha
marry	ማግባት	magibati
master	ባለቤት	balebēti
material	ቁሳዊ	k'usawī
May	ግንቦት	giniboti
mayor	ከንቲባ	kenitība
mean	ማለት	maleti
measurement	መmeasureን	memet'eni
medicine	መድሃኒት	medihanīti
melt	ቀለጠ	k'elet'e
metal	ብረት	bireti
meter	መቀጠሪያ	mek'ut'erīya
milk	ወተት	weteti
million	ሚሊዮን	mīlīyoni
minute	ደቂቃ	dek'īk'a
miscellaneous	ልዩ ልዩ	liyu liyu
mix	ደባለቀ	debalek'e
mix	ደባለቀ	debalek'e
Monday	ሰኞ	senyo
money	ገንዘብ	genizebi
monkey	ዝንጀሮ	zinijero
month	ወር	weri
moon	ጨረቃ	ch'erek'a
morning	ጠዋት	t'ewati
mother	እናት	inati
mountain	ተራራ	terara
mouse	አይጥ	āyit'i

mouth	አፍ	āfi
movie	ፊልም	fīlimi
murder	ግድያ	gidiya
music	ሙዚቃ	muzīk'a
musical	የሙዚቃ	yemuzīk'a
narrow	ጠባብ	t'ebabi
nature	ፍጥረት	fit'ireti
near	ቅርብ	k'iribi
neck	አንገት	ānigeti
needle	መርፌ	merifē
neighbor	ጎረቤት	gorebēti
network	አውታረ መረብ	āwitare merebi
new	አዲስ	ādīsi
newspaper	ጋዜጣ	gazēt'a
nice	ጥሩ	t'iru
night	ለሊት	lelīti
nine	ዘጠኝ	zet'enyi
nineteen	አስራ ዘጠኝ	āsira zet'enyi
ninety	ዘጠና	zet'ena
no	አይ	āyi
north	ሰሜን	semēni
nose	አፍንጫ	āfinich'a
note	ማስታወሻ	masitawesha
November	ህዳር	hidari
nuclear	ኑክሊየር	nukilīyeri
numbers	ቁጥሮች	k'ut'irochi
ocean	ውቅያኖስ	wik'iyanosi
October	ጥቅምት	t'ik'imiti
office	ቢሮ	bīro
oil	ዘይት	zeyiti

old	አሮጌ	ārogē
one	አንድ	ānidi
one hundred	አንድ መቶ	ānidi meto
one hundred thousand	አንድ መቶ ሺሕ	ānidi meto shīhi
one thousand	አንድ ሺህ	ānidi shīhi
one thousand and one	አንድ ሺህ አንድ	ānidi shīhi ānidi
open	ከፈት	kifeti
orange	ብርቱካናማ	biritukanama
our	የኛ	yenya
outside	ውጭ	wich'i
page	ገጽ	gets'i
pain	ሕመም	himemi
paint	ቀለም	k'elemi
pants	ሱሪ	surī
paper	ወረቀት	werek'eti
parent	ወላጅ	welaji
park	መናፈሻ	menafesha
parrot	በቅበቃ	bek'ibek'a
pass	ማለፍ	malefi
patient	ትዕግሥተኛ	ti'igišitenya
pattern	ጥለት	t'ileti
pay	መክፈል	mekifeli
peace	ሰላም	selami
pen	ብዕር	bi'iri
pencil	እርሳስ	irisasi
people	ሕዝብ	hizibi
person	ሰው	sewi
phone	ስልክ	siliki

photograph	ፎቶግራፍ	fotogirafi
piece	ቁራጭ	k'urach'i
pig	አሳማ	āsama
pink	ብሩህ ቀይ	biruhi k'eyi
plane	አውሮፕላን	āwiropilani
plant	ተክል	tekili
plastic	ፕላስቲክ	pilasitīki
plate	ሳህን	šahini
play	ይጫወታሉ	yich'awetalu
player	ተጫዋች	tech'awachi
pocket	ኪስ	kīsi
poison	መርዝ	merizi
police	ፖሊስ	polīsi
pool	መዋኛ	mewanya
poor	ድኻ	diḫa
pork	ያሳማ ሥጋ	yašama šiga
portrait	የቁም	yek'umi
pound	ፓውንድ	pawunidi
pray	ጸለየ	ts'eleye
president	ፕሬዚዳንት	pirēzīdaniti
price	ዋጋ	waga
priest	ቄስ	k'ēsi
prison	እስር ቤት	isiri bēti
program	ፕሮግራም	pirogirami
pronoun	ተዉላጠ ስም	tewulat'e simi
pull	ጎተተ	gotete
push	ገፉ	gefu
queen	ንግሥት	nigišiti
quiet	ጸጥ ያለ	ts'et'i yale
race	ዘር	zeri

race	ዘር	zeri
radio	ራዲዮን	radīyoni
rain	ዝናብ	zinabi
red	ቀይ	k'eyi
relationship	ግንኙነት	gininyuneti
religion	ሃይማኖት	hayimanoti
reporter	ጋዜጠኛ	gazēt'enya
restaurant	ምግብ ቤት	migibi bēti
rice	ሩዝ	ruzi
rich	ሀብታም	hābitami
right	ቀኝ	k'enyi
right	ቀኝ	k'enyi
ring	ቀለበት	k'elebeti
river	ወንዝ	wenizi
road	መንገድ	menigedi
roof	ጣራ	t'ara
room	ክፍል	kifili
root	ሥር	širi
run	ሩጫ	ruch'a
sad	መከፋት	mekefati
salt	ጨው	ch'ewi
sand	አሸዋ	āshewa
Saturday	ቅዳሜ	k'idamē
school	ትምህርት ቤት	timihiriti bēti
science	ሳይንስ	sayinisi
scorpion	ጊንጥ	gīnit'i
screen	ስክሪን	sikirīni
sea	ባሕር	bahiri
season	ወቅት	wek'iti

seasonal	ወቅታዊ	wek'itawī
second	ሁለተኛ	huletenya
secretary	ጸሐፊ	ts'eḥāfī
see	ተመልከት	temeliketi
seed	ዘር	zeri
sell	መሸጥ	meshet'i
September	መስከረም	mesikeremi
seven	ሰባት	sebati
seventeen	አስራ ሰባት	āsira sebati
seventy	ሰባ	seba
shake	ተንቀጠቀጠ	tenik'et'ek'et'e
shallow	ጥልቅ ያልሆነ	t'ilik'i yalihone
she	እርስዋ	irisiwa
sheep	በግ	begi
ship	መርከብ	merikebi
shirt	ሸሚዝ	shemīzi
shoe	ጫማ	ch'ama
shoot	ተኮሰ	tekose
short	አጭር	āch'iri
shoulder	ትከሻ	tikesha
sick	የታመመ	yetameme
side	ወገን	wegeni
sign	ምልክት	milikiti
silver	ብር	biri
sing	ዘምሩ	zemiru
sister	እህት	ihiti
sit	ቁጭ	k'uch'i
six	ስድስት	sidisiti
sixteen	አስራ ስድስት	āsira sidisiti
sixty	ስልሳ	silisa

skin	ቆዳ	k'oda
skirt	ጉርድ ቀሚስ	guridi k'emīsi
sky	ሰማይ	semayi
sleep	እንቅልፍ	inik'ilifi
slow	ዝግ ያለ	zigi yale
small	ትንሽ	tinishi
smell	ሽታ	shita
smile	ፈገግታ	fegegita
snake	እባብ	ibabi
snow	በረዶ	beredo
soap	ሳሙና	samuna
society	ማኅበር	maḫiberi
soft	ለስላሳ	lesilasa
soil	አፈር	āferi
soldier	ወታደር	wetaderi
son	ወንድ ልጅ	wenidi liji
song	ዘፈን	zefeni
sound	ጤናማ	t'ēnama
soup	ሾርባ	shoriba
south	ደቡብ	debubi
space	ቦታ	bota
speak	መናገር	menageri
spoon	ማንካ	manika
sport	ስፖርት	siporiti
spring	ምንጭ	minich'i
spring	ምንጭ	minich'i
square	አራት ማዕዘን	ārati ma'izeni
stain	እድፍ	idifi

stand	ቆም	k'ome
star	ኮከብ	kokebi
station	መሳፈሪያ	mešaferīya
stomach	ሆድ	hodi
stone	ድንጋይ	dinigayi
stop	ተው	tewe
store	መደብር	medebiri
story	ታሪክ	tarīki
straight	ቀጥ ያለ	k'et'i yale
street	መንገድ	menigedi
strong	ጠንካራ	t'enikara
student	ተማሪ	temarī
sugar	ሱካር	sukari
suit	ሙሉ ልብስ	mulu libisi
summer	በጋ	bega
sun	ጸሐይ	ts'eḥāyi
Sunday	እሁድ	ihudi
sweat	ላብ	labi
swim	ዋኘ	wanye
table	ጠረጴዛ	t'erep'ēza
tall	ረጅም	rejimi
taste	ጣዕት	t'a'iti
tea	ሻይ	shayi
teach	ማስተማር	masitemari
teacher	አስተማሪ	āsitemarī
team	ቡድን	budini
tear	እንባ	'iniba
technology	ቴክኖሎጂ	tēkinolojī
teeth	ጥርስ	t'irisi
telephone	ስልክ	siliki

television	ቴሌቪዥን	tēlēvīzhini
temperature	ትኩሳት	tikusati
ten	አስር	āsiri
theater	ትያትር ቤት	tiyatiri bēti
Them	እነሱን	inesuni
They	እነሱ	inesu
thick	ወፍራም	wefirami
thigh	ጭን	ch'ini
thin	ቀጭን	k'ech'ini
think	ማሰብ	masebi
thirteen	አስራ ሶስት	āsira sositi
thirty	ሰላሳ	selasa
three	ሶስት	sositi
throat	ጉሮሮ	guroro
throw	መወርወር	meweriweri
thumb	አውራ ጣት	āwura t'ati
Thursday	ሐሙስ	ḥāmusi
ticket	ቲኬት	tīkēti
tight	ጠባብ	t'ebabi
time	ጊዜ	gīzē
tire	ጎማ	goma
today	ዛሬ	zarē
toe	የእግር ጣት	ye'igiri t'ati
toilet	ሽንት ቤት	shiniti bēti
tomorrow	ነገ	nege
tongue	ምላስ	milasi
tool	መሣሪያ	mešarīya
tooth	ጥርስ	t'irisi
top	ጫፍ	ch'afi

touch	ነካ	neka
town	ከተማ	ketema
train	ባቡር	baburi
transportation	መጓጓዣ	megwagwazha
tree	ዛፍ	zafi
truck	ትራክ	tiraki
T-shirt	ቲ-ቲሸርት	tī - tīsheriti
Tuesday	ማክሰኞ	makisenyo
turn	ማዞሪያ	mazorīya
turtle	ኤሊ	ēlī
twelve	አስራ ሁለት	āsira huleti
twenty	ሃያ	haya
twenty-eight	ሃያ-ስምንት	haya - siminiti
twenty-five	ሃያ አምስት	haya āmisiti
twenty-four	ሃያ አራት	haya ārati
twenty-nine	ሃያ ዘጠኝ	haya zet'enyi
twenty-one	ሃያ አንድ	haya ānidi
twenty-seven	ሃያ ሰባት	haya sebati
twenty-six	ሃያ ስድስት	haya sidisiti
twenty-three	ሃያ ሶስት	haya sositi
twenty-two	ሃያ ሁለት	haya huleti
two	ሁለት	huleti
ugly	ፉንጋ	funiga
university	ዩኒቨርሲቲ	yunīverisītī
up	እስከ	isike
up	እስከ	isike
valley	ሸለቆ	shelek'o
Verb	ግሥ	giši
victim	ሰለባ	seleba
voice	ድምጽ	dimits'i

vote	ድምጽ	dimits'i
vowel	ቫወል	vaweli
waiter	አሳላፊ	āsalafī
walk	መራመድ	meramedi
wall	ግድግዳ	gidigida
war	ጦርነት	t'orineti
warm	ሙቅ	muk'i
wash	ማጠብ	mat'ebi
watch	ይመልከቱ	yimeliketu
water	ውሃ	wiha
wave	ማዕበል	ma'ibeli
we	እኛ	inya
weak	ደካማ	dekama
wear	መልበስ	melibesi
wedding	ሰርግ	serigi
Wednesday	እሮብ	irobi
week	ሳምንት	saminiti
weight	ሚዛን	mīzani
west	ምዕራብ	mi'irabi
wet	እርጥብ	irit'ibi
whiskey	ውስኪ	wisikī
white	ነጭ	nech'i
wide	ሰፊ	sefī
wife	ሚስት	mīsiti
win	ማሸነፍ	mashenefi
wind	ነፋስ	nefasi
window	መስኮት	mesikoti
wine	የወይን ጠጅ	yeweyini t'eji
wing	ክንፍ	kinifi

winter	ክረምት	kiremiti
woman	ሴት	sēti
wood	እንጨት	inich'eti
work	ሥራ	šira
world	ዓለም	'alemi
write	ጻፈ	ts'afe
yard	ያርድ	yaridi
year	አመት	āmeti
yellow	ቢጫ	bīch'a
yes	አዎ	āwo
yesterday	ትናንትና	tinanitina
you	አንተ	ānite
young	ወጣት	wet'ati
zebra	የሜዳ አህያ	yemēda āhiya
zero	ዜሮ	zēro

የአማርኛ / እንግሊዝኛ / በቋንቋ

ላም	cow	lami
ቀጭኔ	giraffe	k'ech'inē
በቅቢቃ	parrot	bek'ibek'a
በግ	sheep	begi
ቢራቢሮ	butterfly	bīrabīro
ነሥር	eagle	neširi
አህያ	donkey	āhiya
አሳማ	pig	āsama
እንቁራሪት	frog	ānik'urarīti
አንበሳ	lion	ānibesa
አይጥ	mouse	āyit'i
ኤሊ	turtle	ēlī
እባብ	snake	ibabi
እንስሳት	**Animals**	inisisati
ወፍ	bird	wefi
ውሻ	dog	wisha
ዝሆን	elephant	zihoni
ዝንጀሮ	monkey	zinijero
ዝዬ	goose	ziyī
የሜዳ አህያ	zebra	yemēda āhiya
ዳክዬ	duck	dakiye
ድመት	cat	dimeti
ገመሬ	gorilla	gemerē
ጊንጥ	scorpion	gīnit'i
ፈረስ	horse	feresi
መርከብ	ship	merikebi
መንገድ	road	menigedi
መኪና	car	mekīna

መጓጓዣ	transportation	megwagwazha
ምልክት	sign	milikiti
ቢስክሌት	bicycle	bīsikilēti
ባቡር	train	baburi
ቤንዚን	gasoline	bēnizīni
ተወ	stop	tewe
ትራክ	truck	tiraki
አውቶቡስ	bus	āwitobusi
ድራይቭ	drive	dirayivi
ጀልባ	boat	jeliba
ጎማ	tire	goma
ሆቴል	hotel	hotēli
ሙሣፈሪያ	station	mešaferīya
መናፈሻ	park	menafesha
መንገድ	street	menigedi
ምግብ ቤት	restaurant	migibi bēti
ቢሮ	office	bīro
ቤተ መጻሕፍት	library	bēte mets'aḥifiti
ቤተ ክርስትያን	church	bēte kirisitiyani
ትምህርት ቤት	school	timihiriti bēti
ትያትር ቤት	theater	tiyatiri bēti
አካባቢ	location	ākababī
አገር	country	āgeri
አስር ቤት	prison	isiri bēti
እርሻ	farm	irisha
ከተማ	city	ketema
ከተማ	town	ketema
ካርታ	map	karita
የባህር ዳርቻ	beach	yebahiri daricha
ዩኒቨርሲቲ	university	yunīverisītī

ገበያ	market	gebeya
ልብስ	clothing	libisi
ልብስ	dress	libisi
መልበስ	wear	melibesi
ሙሉ ልብስ	suit	mulu libisi
ሱሪ	pants	surī
ሽሚዝ	shirt	shemīzi
ቀበቶ	belt	k'ebeto
ቆብ	cap	k'obi
ባርኔጣ	hat	barinēt'a
ቦት ጫማ	boot	boti ch'ama
ቲ-ቲሸርት	T-shirt	tī - tīsheriti
ካፖርት	coat	kaporiti
የሴቶች ሽሚዝ	blouse	yesētochi shemīzi
ጂንስ	jeans	jīnisi
ጉርድ ቀሚስ	skirt	guridi k'emīsi
ጉርድ ኮት	jacket	guridi koti
ጓንት	gloves	gwaniti
ጫማ	shoe	ch'ama
ሰማያዊ	blue	semayawī
ቀለም	color	k'elemi
ቀይ	red	k'eyi
ቅባት	cream	k'ibati
ብሩህ ቀይ	pink	biruhi k'eyi
ብናማ	brown	binama
ነጭ	white	nech'i
አረንጓዴ	green	ārenigwadē
ወርቅ	gold	werik'i
ግልጽ	clear	gilits'i

ግራጫ	gray	girach'a
ጥቁር	black	t'ik'uri
ጥቁር	dark	t'ik'uri
ሕዝብ	people	ḥizibi
ሕፃን	child	ḥits'ani
ሴት ልጅ	girl	sēti liji
ቄስ	priest	k'ēsi
ንጉሥ	king	niguši
ንግሥት	queen	nigišiti
አስተማሪ	teacher	āsitemarī
አዋቂ	adult	āwak'ī
ወንድ ልጅ	boy	wenidi liji
ጎረቤት	neighbor	gorebēti
ሥራ	Job	šira
ሥራ	work	šira
ተማሪ	student	temarī
ነገረፈጅ	lawyer	negerefeji
አሳላፊ	waiter	āsalafī
አርኪቴክት	architect	ārikītēkiti
ወታደር	soldier	wetaderi
የቴአትር ተጫዋች	actor	yetē'ātiri tech'awachi
የቴአትር ተጫዋች	actress	yetē'ātiri tech'awachi
ደናሽ	dancer	denashi
ዳቦ ጋጋሪ	baker	dabo gagarī
ጋዜጠኛ	reporter	gazēt'enya
ጸሐፊ	secretary	ts'eḥāfī
ፕሬዚዳንት	president	pirēzīdaniti
ፖሊስ	police	polīsi
ማኅበር	society	maḥiberi
ምርጫ	election	mirich'a

እጩ	candidate	ich'u
ከንቲባ	mayor	kenitība
የምርጫ ወረቀት	ballot	yemirich'a werek'eti
ይጫወታሉ	play	yich'awetalu
ዴሞክራሲ	democracy	dēmokirasī
ድምጽ	vote	dimits'i
ጦርነት	war	t'orineti
መያዣ	easel	meyazha
ሠዓሊ	artist	še'alī
ሥነ ጥበብ	art	šine t'ibebi
ረቂቅ	abstract	rek'īk'i
ባለቤት	master	balebēti
የሥዕል ማሳያ አዳራሽ	gallery	yeši'ili masaya ādarashi
የቁም	portrait	yek'umi
ሻይ	tea	shayi
ቡና	coffee	buna
ቢራ	beer	bīra
አልኮል	alcohol	ālikoli
ወተት	milk	weteti
ውሃ	water	wiha
ውስኪ	whiskey	wisikī
የወይን ጠጅ	wine	yeweyini t'eji
ጠጣ	drink	t'et'a
ጭማቂ	juice	ch'imak'ī
ሎሚ	lemon	lomī
ሙብላት	eat	mebilati
ሙዝ	banana	muzi
ማንካ	spoon	manika
ምሳ	lunch	misa

የእንግሊዝኛ / አማርኛ የአነጋገር መዝገበ ቃላት   145

ምግብ	food	migibi
ሱካር	sugar	sukari
ሣህን	plate	šahini
ሩዝ	rice	ruzi
ሾርባ	soup	shoriba
ቁርስ	breakfast	k'urisi
ቅቤ	butter	k'ibē
በረዶ	ice	beredo
በቆሎ	corn	bek'olo
ቢላዋ	knife	bīlawa
ብር	silver	biri
ብርቱካናማ	orange	biritukanama
ዓሣ	fish	'aša
እራት	dinner	irati
እንቁላል	egg	inik'ulali
ኬክ	cake	kēki
የበሬ ሥጋ	beef	yeberē šiga
የደረቀ አይብ	cheese	yederek'e āyibi
ያሣማ ሥጋ	pork	yašama šiga
ዳቦ	bread	dabo
ጨው	salt	ch'ewi
ጫጩት	chicken	ch'ach'īti
ፓም	apple	pami
ሹካ	fork	vuka
መስኮት	window	mesikoti
መብራት	lamp	mebirati
መኖሪያ ቤት	home	menorīya bēti
መኝታ ቤት	bedroom	menyita bēti
ሽንት ቤት	toilet	shiniti bēti
ቁልፍ	key	k'ulifi

ቁልፍ	lock	k'ulifi
በር	door	beri
ቤት	house	bēti
ክፍል	room	kifili
ወምበር	chair	wemiberi
ወጥ ቤት	kitchen	wet'i bēti
ውስጥ	inside	wisit'i
ውጪ	outside	wich'i
የአትክልት	garden	ye'ātikiliti
ያርድ	yard	yaridi
ጠረጴዛ	table	t'erep'ēza
ጣራ	ceiling	t'ara
ጣራ	roof	t'ara
ላፕቶፕ	laptop	lapitopi
ስልክ	phone	siliki
ስልክ	telephone	siliki
ራዲዮን	radio	radīyoni
በረዶ	snow	beredo
ቴሌቪዥን	television	tēlēvīzhini
ኤሌክትሮኒክስ	electronics	ēlēkitironīkisi
ካሜራ	camera	kamēra
ኮምፒዩተር	computer	komipiyuteri
ሐይቅ	lake	ḥāyik'i
መሬት	earth	merēti
መሬት	ground	merēti
መዋኛ	pool	mewanya
ሙቅ	hot	muk'i
ማዕበል	wave	ma'ibeli

ሰማይ	sky	semayi
ሥር	root	širi
ሸለቆ	valley	shelek'o
ቅጠል	leaf	k'it'eli
ባሕር	sea	baḥiri
ቦታ	space	bota
ተራራ	mountain	terara
ተክል	plant	tekili
አሸዋ	sand	āshewa
አፈር	soil	āferi
ዓለም	world	'alemi
ኮረብታ	hill	korebita
ኮከብ	star	kokebi
ወንዝ	river	wenizi
ውቅያኖስ	ocean	wik'iyanosi
ዘር	seed	zeri
ዛፍ	tree	zafi
ደሴት	island	desēti
ደረቅ	**dry**	derek'i
ደን	forest	deni
ድንጋይ	stone	dinigayi
ጨረቃ	moon	ch'erek'a
ጸሐይ	sun	ts'eḥāyi
ፍጥረት	nature	fit'ireti
መመጠን	measurement	memet'eni
መቀጠሪያ	meter	mek'ut'erīya
ሚዛን	weight	mīzani
ሳንቲሜትር	centimeter	sanitīmētiri
ትኩሳት	temperature	tikusati
አራት ማዕዘን	square	ārati ma'izeni

ኢንች	inch	īnichi
ግራም	kilogram	girami
ፓዉንድ	pound	pawunidi
ምስራቅ	east	misirak'i
ምዕራብ	west	mi'irabi
ሰሜን	north	semēni
ሩቅ	far	ruk'i
ቀኝ	right	k'enyi
ቅርብ	near	k'iribi
ታች	bottom	tachi
እስከ	up	isike
ወደታች	down	wedetachi
ወገን	side	wegeni
ዝቅ ያለ	low	zik'i yale
ደቡብ	south	debubi
ግራ	left	gira
ምንጯ	spring	minich'i
በልግ	autumn	beligi
ቢጋ	summer	bega
ክረምት	winter	kiremiti
ወቅት	season	wek'iti
መጣጠቢያ ክፍል	bathroom	met'at'ebīya kifili
ሳሙና	soap	samuna
ሃምሳ	fifty	hamisa
ሃያ	twenty	haya
ሃያ ሁለት	twenty-two	haya huleti
ሃያ ሰባት	twenty-seven	haya sebati
ሃያ ስድስት	twenty-six	haya sidisiti
ሃያ ሶስት	twenty-three	haya sositi

ሃያ አምስት	twenty-five	haya āmisiti
ሃያ አራት	twenty-four	haya ārati
ሃያ አንድ	twenty-one	haya ānidi
ሃያ ዘጠኝ	twenty-nine	haya zet'enyi
ሃያ-ስምንት	twenty-eight	haya - siminiti
ሁለት	two	huleti
ሚሊዮን	million	mīlīyoni
ሰላሳ	thirty	selasa
ሰማንያ	eighty	semaniya
ሰባ	seventy	seba
ሰባት	seven	sebati
ስልሳ	sixty	silisa
ስምት	eight	simiti
ስድስት	six	sidisiti
ሶስት	three	sositi
ቁጥሮች	numbers	k'ut'irochi
ቢሊዮን	billion	bīlīyoni
ተጎዳሁ:	count	tegodahu:
አምስት	five	āmisiti
አስራ ሁለት	twelve	āsira huleti
አስራ ሰባት	seventeen	āsira sebati
አስራ ስምንት	eighteen	āsira siminiti
አስራ ስድስት	sixteen	āsira sidisiti
አስራ ሶስት	thirteen	āsira sositi
አስራ አምስት	fifteen	āsira āmisiti
አስራ አራት	fourteen	āsira ārati
አስራ አንድ	eleven	āsira ānidi
አስራ ዘጠኝ	nineteen	āsira zet'enyi
አስር	ten	āsiri
አራት	four	ārati

አርባ	forty	āriba
አንድ	one	ānidi
አንድ መቶ	one hundred	ānidi meto
አንድ መቶ ሺሕ	one hundred thousand	ānidi meto shīḫi
አንድ ሺህ	one thousand	ānidi shīḫi
አንድ ሺህ አንድ	one thousand and one	ānidi shīḫi ānidi
ዘጠና	ninety	zet'ena
ዘጠኝ	nine	zet'enyi
ዜሮ	zero	zēro
ሐምሌ	July	hāmilē
ህዳር	November	hidari
መስከረም	September	mesikeremi
መጋቢት	March	megabīti
ሚያዚያ	April	mīyazīya
ሰኔ	June	senē
ቀን	date	k'eni
ታህሳስ	December	tahisasi
ነሐሴ	August	neḥāsē
ወር	month	weri
የካቲት	February	yekatīti
ግንቦት	May	giniboti
ጥር	January	t'iri
ጥቅምት	October	t'ik'imiti
ሐሙስ	Thursday	ḥāmusi
ማክሰኞ	Tuesday	makisenyo
ሰኞ	Monday	senyo
ሳምንት	week	saminiti

ቀን	day	k'eni
ቅዳሜ	Saturday	k'idamē
አርብ	Friday	āribi
እሁድ	Sunday	ihudi
እሮብ	Wednesday	irobi
ክንፍ	wing	kinifi
ለሊት	night	lelīti
ምሽት	evening	mishiti
ሰአት	hour	se'āti
ሰዓት	clock	se'ati
ትናንትና	yesterday	tinanitina
ነገ	tomorrow	nege
አመት	year	āmeti
ከሰአት	afternoon	kese'āti
ዛሬ	today	zarē
ደቂቃ	minute	dek'īk'a
ጊዜ	time	gīzē
ጠዋት	morning	t'ewati
ሆድ	stomach	hodi
ላብ	sweat	labi
ልብ	heart	libi
ራስ	head	rasi
ቆዳ	skin	k'oda
ትልቅ ሣጥን	chest	tilik'i šat'ini
ትከሻ	shoulder	tikesha
አንገት	neck	ānigeti
አእምሮ	brain	ā'imiro
አካል	body	ākali

English / Amharic Dictionary

አውራ ጣት	thumb	āwura t'ati
አገጭ	chin	āgech'i
አጥንት	bone	āt'initi
አፍንጫ	nose	āfinich'a
ዓይን	eye	'ayini
እጅ	hand	iji
እግር	foot	igiri
እግር	leg	igiri
ክንድ	arm	kinidi
ክንድ	elbow	kinidi
የእግር ጣት	toe	ye'igiri t'ati
ጉልበት	knee	gulibeti
ጉሮሮ	throat	guroro
ጉንጮቹ	cheeks	gunich'ochu
ጠጉር	hair	t'eguri
ጣቶች	fingers	t'atochi
ጥርስ	teeth	t'irisi
ጥርስ	tooth	t'irisi
ጭን	thigh	ch'ini
ፊት	face	fīti
ሐኪም ቤት	hospital	ḥākīmi bēti
ሕመም	pain	ḥimemi
መርዝ	poison	merizi
መድሃኒት	drug	medihanīti
መድሃኒት	medicine	medihanīti
መግደል	kill	megideli
ትዕግሥተኛ	patient	ti'igišitenya

ዕውር	blind	'iwiri
የሞተ	dead	yemote
የታመመ	sick	yetameme
ደም	blood	demi
ደንቆሮ	deaf	denik'oro
ጆሮ	ear	joro
ጉዳት	injury	gudati
ጤናማ	healthy	t'ēnama
መሸጥ	sell	meshet'i
መደብር	store	medebiri
ርካሽ	cheap	rikashi
ባንክ	bank	baniki
ዋጋ	price	waga
ዶላር	dollar	dolari
ገንዘብ	money	genizebi
ሕፃን	child	ḥits'ani
ሚስት	wife	mīsiti
ማግባት	marry	magibati
ሰርግ	wedding	serigi
ሰው	man	sewi
ሴት	female	sēti
ሴት	woman	sēti
ሴት ልጅ	daughter	sēti liji
ሴት ልጅ	girl	sēti liji
ሴት አያት	grandmother	sēti āyati
ባል	husband	bali
ቤተሰብ	family	bēteseli
ተባዕት	male	teba'iti
አባት	father	ābati
እህት	sister	ihiti

English / Amharic Dictionary

እናት	mother	inati
ወላጅ	parent	welaji
ወንድ ልጅ	son	wenidi liji
ወንድ አያት	grandfather	wenidi āyati
ወንድም	brother	wenidimi
ጋብቻ	marriage	gabicha
ግንኙነት	relationship	gininyuneti
እንደምን አደርክ	good morning	inidemini āderiki
ዘለለ	jump	zelele
ደባለቀ	mix	debalek'e
ሀብታም	rich	hābitami
ሐኪም	doctor	ḫākīmi
ኃይል	energy	ḫayili
ሃይማኖት	religion	hayimanoti
ሁለተኛ	second	huletenya
ሂሳቡ	bill	hīsabu
ሕልም	dream	hilimi
ሕንፃ	building	ḫinits'a
ሕዋስ	cell	hiwasi
ሕዝብ	crowd	hizibi
ሕፃን ልጅ	baby	hits'ani liji
ለመግዛት	buy	lemegizati
ለመግዛት	buy	lemegizati
ለስላሳ	soft	lesilasa
ላም	cow	lami
ልዩ ልዩ	miscellaneous	liyu liyu
መልመጃ	exercise	melimeja
መማር	learn	memari
መምታት	beat	memitati

መሞት	die	memoti
መሳል	draw	mesali
መሳም	kiss	mesami
መሣሪያ	instrument	mešarīya
መሣሪያ	tool	mešarīya
መራመድ	walk	meramedi
መርፌ	needle	merifē
መሸከም	carry	meshekemi
መብራት	light	mebirati
መናገር	speak	menageri
መንግሥተ ሰማያት	heaven	menigišite semayati
መኖሪያ ቤት	apartment	menorīya bēti
መኖሪያ ቤት	flat	menorīya bēti
መከፋት	sad	mekefati
መኪና	engine	mekīna
መኪና	engine	mekīna
መክፈል	pay	mekifeli
መወርወር	throw	meweriweri
መዝገበ ቃላት	dictionary	mezigebe k'alati
መዳብ	copper	medabi
መገንባት	build	megenibati
መጥፎ	bad	met'ifo
መጽሐፍ	book	mets'iḥāfi
መጽሔት	magazine	mets'iḥēti
ሙቀት	heat	muk'eti
ሙቅ	warm	muk'i
ሙዚቃ	music	muzīk'a
ማለት	mean	maleti
ማለፍ	pass	malefi

ማሰብ	think	masebi
ማስተማር	teach	masitemari
ማስታወሻ	note	masitawesha
ማሸነፍ	win	mashenefi
ማዕዘን	corner	ma'izeni
ማዞሪያ	turn	mazorīya
ማግኘት	find	maginyeti
ማጠብ	wash	mat'ebi
ምላስ	tongue	milasi
ምስል	image	misili
ምንጭ	spring	minich'i
ምግብ	feed	migibi
ምግብ	food	migibi
ሞት	death	moti
ሰለባ	victim	seleba
ሰላም	peace	selami
ሰማ	hear	sema
ሰቀለ	hang	sek'ele
ሰው	person	sewi
ሠፈር	camp	šeferi
ሰፊ	wide	sefī
ሲኒ	cup	sīnī
ሲኦል	hell	sī'oli
ሣር	grass	šari
ሳቅ	laugh	sak'i
ሳይንስ	science	sayinisi
ሳጥን	box	sat'ini
ስምምነት	contract	simimineti
ሥራ	job	šira

ስክሪን	screen	sikirīni
ስጦታ	gift	sit'ota
ስፖርት	sport	siporiti
ረጅም	long	rejimi
ረጅም	tall	rejimi
ሩጫ	run	ruch'a
ሸክላ	clay	shekila
ሽታ	smell	shita
ቀለም	paint	k'elemi
ቀለበት	ring	k'elebeti
ቀለጠ	melt	k'elet'e
ቀኝ	right	k'enyi
ቀዳዳ	hole	k'edada
ቀጥ ያለ	straight	k'et'i yale
ቀጭን	thin	k'ech'ini
ቁሳዊ	material	k'usawī
ቁራጭ	piece	k'urach'i
ቁሻሻ	dirty	k'ushasha
ቁጭ	sit	k'uch'i
ቅጽሎችን	adjectives	k'its'ilochini
ቆመ	stand	k'ome
ቆረጠ	cut	k'oret'e
ቆንጆ	beautiful	k'onijo
ቆፈረ	dig	k'ofere
በ	by	be
በሕይወት	alive	behiyiweti
በሽታ	disease	beshita
በታላቅ	loud	betalak'i
በፍጥነት	fast	befit'ineti
ቡና ቤት	bar	buna bēti

ቡድን	team	budini
ቢጫ	yellow	bīch'a
ብረት	metal	bireti
ብርድ	cold	biridi
ብርጭቆ	glass	birich'ik'o
ብዕር	pen	bi'iri
ቦርሳ	bag	borisa
ተመልከት	see	temeliketi
ተንቀጠቀጠ	shake	tenik'et'ek'et'e
ተከተል	follow	teketeli
ተኮስ	shoot	tekose
ተዉላጠ ስም	pronoun	tewulat'e simi
ተጫዋች	player	tech'awachi
ቲኬት	ticket	tīkēti
ታሪክ	story	tarīki
ቴክኖሎጂ	technology	tēkinolojī
ትልቅ	big	tilik'i
ትንሽ	small	tinishi
ትግል	fight	tigili
ነካ	touch	neka
ነጥብ	dot	net'ibi
ነፋስ	wind	nefasi
ኑክሊየር	nuclear	nukilīyeri
ንጹሕ	clean	nits'uḫi
አልማዝ	diamond	ālimazi
አልጋ	bed	āliga
አምላክ	God	āmilaki
አሳንሰር	lift	āsaniseri
አስተዳዳሪ	manager	āsitedadarī

አሮጌ	old	ārogē
አቅጣጫዎች	Directions	āk'it'ach'awochi ~
አበባ	flower	ābeba
አንተ	you	ānite
አዋለ	explode	āwale
አውሮፕላን	plane	āwiropilani
አውታረ መረብ	network	āwitare merebi
አዎ	yes	āwo
አየር	air	āyeri
አይ	no	āyi
አዲስ	new	ādīsi
አጭር	short	āch'iri
አፈር	dust	āferi
አፍ	mouth	āfi
ኢጓና	iguana	īgiwana
እሳት	fire	isati
እስከ	up	isike
እረፍት	break	irefiti
እርሱ	he	irisu
እርሳስ	pencil	irisasi
እርስዋ	she	irisiwa
እርጥብ	wet	irit'ibi
እነሱ	They	inesu
እነሱን	Them	inesuni
እኔ	I	inē
እንቅልፍ	sleep	inik'ilifi
እንባ	tear	'iniba
እንጨት	wood	inich'eti
እኛ	we	inya

እያደገ	grow	iyadege
እድፍ	stain	idifi
ከባድ	heavy	kebadi
ከንፈር	lip	keniferi
ከፍ ያለ	high	kefi yale
ኪስ	pocket	kīsi
ካርድ	card	karidi
ክበብ	circle	kibebi
ክፈት	open	kifeti
ኳስ	ball	kwasi
ወለል	floor	weleli
ወረቀት	paper	werek'eti
ወርቅ	gold	werik'i
ወቅታዊ	seasonal	wek'itawī
ወደኋላ	back	wedeḫwala
ወደኋላ	back	wedeḫwala
ወደቀ	fall	wedek'e
ወጣት	young	wet'ati
ወጥ ቤት ሴት	cook	wet'i bēti sēti
ወፍራም	thick	wefirami
ዋኘ	swim	wanye
ውድ	expensive	widi
ዘምሩ	sing	zemiru
ዘር	race	zeri
ዘር	race	zeri
ዘይት	oil	zeyiti
ዘፈን	song	zefeni
ዝምብ	fly	zimibi

የእንግሊዝኛ / አማርኛ የአነጋገር መዝገበ ቃላት 161

ዝናብ	rain	zinabi
ዝግ ያለ	slow	zigi yale
የሙዚቃ	musical	yemuzīk'a
የተፈታ	loose	yetefeta
የኛ	our	yenya
የአልኮል መጠጥ	alcoholic drink	ye'ālikoli met'et'i
የአውሮፕላን ማረፊያ	airport	ye'āwiropilani marefīya
ያቃጥለዋል	burn	yak'at'ilewali
ያዘ	catch	yaze
ያጣሉ	lose	yat'alu
ይህ	it	yihi
ይመልከቱ	watch	yimeliketu
ደሴት	island	desēti
ደስተኛ	happy	desitenya
ደራሲ	author	derasī
ደባለቀ	mix	debalek'e
ደብዳቤ	letter	debidabē
ደካማ	weak	dekama
ዳንስ	dance	danisi
ድላ	club	dila
ድልድይ	bridge	dilidiyi
ድምጽ	voice	dimits'i
ድምጽ ተቀባይ ፊደል	consonant	dimits'i tek'ebayi fīdeli
ድኻ	poor	diẖa
ገጠመ	close	get'eme
ገጽ	page	gets'i
ገፋ	push	gefu
ጋዜጣ	newspaper	gazēt'a

ጋደም ማለት	lie down	gademi maleti
ግማሽ	half	gimashi
ግሥ	Verb	giši
ግድያ	murder	gidiya
ግድግዳ	wall	gidigida
ጎበጠ	bend	gobet'e
ጎተተ	pull	gotete
ጓድ	band	gwadi
ጠርሙዝ	bottle	t'erimuzi
ጠርዝ	edge	t'erizi
ጠበንጃ	gun	t'ebenija
ጠባብ	narrow	t'ebabi
ጠባብ	tight	t'ebabi
ጠንካራ	hard	t'enikara
ጠንካራ	strong	t'enikara
ጢም	beard	t'īmi
ጣት	finger	t'ati
ጣዕት	taste	t'a'iti
ጤናማ	sound	t'ēnama
ጥለት	pattern	t'ileti
ጥልቅ	deep	t'ilik'i
ጥልቅ ያልሆነ	shallow	t'ilik'i yalihone
ጥምዝ	curved	t'imizi
ጥሩ	cool	t'iru
ጥሩ	good	t'iru
ጥሩ	nice	t'iru
ጥሪ	call	t'irī
ጥቁር	dark	t'ik'uri
ጥቃት	attack	t'ik'ati

ጦር ሠራዊት	army	t'ori šerawīti
ጨዋታ	game	ch'ewata
ጫፍ	top	ch'afi
ጭኸ	cry	ch'oẖe
ጸለየ	pray	ts'eleye
ጸጥ ያለ	quiet	ts'et'i yale
ጻፈ	write	ts'afe
ፈን	fan	feni
ፈን	fan	feni
ፈገግታ	smile	fegegita
ፉንጋ	ugly	funiga
ፊልም	movie	fīlimi
ፊት	front	fīti
ፍርድ ቤት	court	firidi bēti
ፍቅር	love	fik'iri
ፎቶግራፍ	photograph	fotogirafi
ፕላስቲክ	plastic	pilasitīki
ፕሮግራም	program	pirogirami
ባወል	vowel	vaweli

bek'wanik'wa / ye'āmarinya / inigilīzinya

'alemi	ዓለም	world
'aša	ዓሣ	fish
'ayini	ዓይን	eye
'iniba	እንባ	tear
'iwiri	እውር	blind
ā'imiro	አአምሮ	brain
ābati	አባት	father
ābeba	አበባ	flower
āch'iri	አጭር	short
ādīsi	አዲስ	new
āferi	አፈር	soil
āferi	አፈር	dust
āfi	አፍ	mouth
āfinich'a	አፍንጫ	nose
āgech'i	አገጭ	chin
āgeri	አገር	country
āhiya	አህያ	donkey
āk'it'ach'awochi ~	አቅጣጫዎች	Directions
ākababī	አካባቢ	location
ākali	አካል	body
āliga	አልጋ	bed
ālikoli	አልኮል	alcohol
ālimazi	አልማዝ	diamond
āmeti	አመት	year
āmilaki	አምላክ	God

āmisiti	አምስት	five
ānibesa	አንበሳ	lion
ānidi	አንድ	one
ānidi meto	አንድ መቶ	one hundred
ānidi meto shīḫi	አንድ መቶ ሺሕ	one hundred thousand
ānidi shīhi	አንድ ሺህ	one thousand
ānidi shīhi ānidi	አንድ ሺህ አንድ	one thousand and one
ānigeti	አንገት	neck
ānik'urarīti	አንቁራሪት	frog
ānite	አንተ	you
ārati	አራት	four
ārati ma'izeni	አራት ማዕዘን	square
ārenigwadē	አረንጓዴ	green
āriba	አርባ	forty
āribi	አርብ	Friday
ārikītēkiti	አርኪቴክት	architect
ārogē	አሮጌ	old
āsalafī	አሳላፊ	waiter
āsama	አሳማ	pig
āsaniseri	አሳንሰር	lift
āshewa	አሸዋ	sand
āsira āmisiti	አስራ አምስት	fifteen
āsira ānidi	አስራ አንድ	eleven
āsira ārati	አስራ አራት	fourteen
āsira huleti	አስራ ሁለት	twelve
āsira sebati	አስራ ሰባት	seventeen
āsira sidisiti	አስራ ስድስት	sixteen
āsira siminiti	አስራ ስምንት	eighteen

āsira sositi	አስራ ሶስት	thirteen
āsira zet'enyi	አስራ ዘጠኝ	nineteen
āsiri	አስር	ten
āsitedadarī	አስተዳዳሪ	manager
āsitemarī	አስተማሪ	teacher
āt'initi	አጥንት	bone
āwak'ī	አዋቂ	adult
āwale	አዋለ	explode
āwiropilani	አውሮፕላን	plane
āwitare merebi	አውታረ መረብ	network
āwitobusi	አውቶቡስ	bus
āwo	አዎ	yes
āwura t'ati	አዉራ ጣት	thumb
āyeri	አየር	air
āyi	አይ	no
āyit'i	አይጥ	mouse
baburi	ባቡር	train
bahiri	ባሕር	sea
balebēti	ባለቤት	master
bali	ባል	husband
baniki	ባንክ	bank
barinēt'a	ባርኔጣ	hat
be	በ	by
befit'ineti	በፍጥነት	fast
bega	በጋ	summer
begi	በግ	sheep
behiyiweti	በሕይወት	alive
bek'ibek'a	በቅብቃ	parrot
bek'olo	በቆሎ	corn

beligi	በልግ	autumn
bēnizīni	ቤንዚን	gasoline
beredo	በረዶ	ice
beredo	በረዶ	snow
beri	በር	door
beshita	በሽታ	disease
betalak'i	በታላቅ	loud
bēte kirisitiyani	ቤተ ክርስትያን	church
bēte mets'aḥifiti	ቤተ መጻሕፍት	library
bētesebi	ቤተሰብ	family
bēti	ቤት	house
bi'iri	ብዕር	pen
bīch'a	ቢጫ	yellow
bīlawa	ቢላዋ	knife
bīlīyoni	ቢሊዮን	billion
binama	ብናማ	brown
bīra	ቢራ	beer
bīrabīro	ቢራቢሮ	butterfly
bireti	ብረት	metal
biri	ብር	silver
birich'ik'o	ብርጭቆ	glass
biridi	ብርድ	cold
biritukanama	ብርቱካናማ	orange
bīro	ቢሮ	office
biruhi k'eyi	ብሩህ ቀይ	pink
bīsikilēti	ቢስክሌት	bicycle
borisa	ቦርሳ	bag
bota	ቦታ	space
boti ch'ama	ቦት ጫማ	boot

budini	ቡዲን	team
buna	ቡና	coffee
buna bēti	ቡና ቤት	bar
ch'ach'īti	ጨጪት	chicken
ch'afi	ጨፍ	top
ch'ama	ጫማ	shoe
ch'erek'a	ጨረቃ	moon
ch'ewata	ጨዋታ	game
ch'ewi	ጨው	salt
ch'imak'ī	ጭማቂ	juice
ch'ini	ጭን	thigh
ch'oẖe	ጭኽ	cry
dabo	ዳቦ	bread
dabo gagarī	ዳቦ ጋጋሪ	baker
dakiye	ዳክየ	duck
danisi	ዳንስ	dance
debalek'e	ደባለቀ	mix
debalek'e	ደባለቀ	mix
debidabē	ደብዳቤ	letter
debubi	ደቡብ	south
dek'īk'a	ደቂቃ	minute
dekama	ደካማ	weak
demi	ደም	**blood**
dēmokirasī	ዴሞክራሲ	democracy
denashi	ደናሽ	dancer
deni	ደን	forest
denik'oro	ደንቆሮ	deaf
derasī	ደራሲ	author
derek'i	ደረቅ	**dry**

desēti	ደሴት	island
desēti	ደሴት	island
desitenya	ደስተኛ	happy
diha	ድኻ	poor
dila	ድላ	club
dilidiyi	ድልድይ	bridge
dimeti	ድመት	cat
dimits'i	ድምጽ	vote
dimits'i	ድምጽ	voice
dimits'i tek'ebayi fīdeli	ድምጽ ተቀባይ ፊደል	consonant
dinigayi	ድንጋይ	stone
dirayivi	ድራይቭ	drive
dolari	ዶላር	dollar
ēlēkitironīkisi	ኤሌክትሮኒክስ	electronics
ēlī	ኤሊ	turtle
fegegita	ፈገግታ	smile
feni	ፈን	fan
feni	ፈን	fan
feresi	ፈረስ	horse
fik'iri	ፍቅር	love
fīlimi	ፊልም	movie
firidi bēti	ፍርድ ቤት	court
fit'ireti	ፍጥረት	nature
fīti	ፊት	face
fīti	ፊት	front
fotogirafi	ፎቶግራፍ	photograph
funiga	ፉንጋ	ugly
gabicha	ጋብቻ	marriage
gademi maleti	ጋደም ማለት	lie down

gazēt'a	ጋዜጣ	newspaper
gazēt'enya	ጋዜጠኛ	reporter
gebeya	ገበያ	market
gefu	ገፉ	push
gemerē	ገመሬ	gorilla
genizebi	ገንዘብ	money
get'eme	ገጠመ	close
gets'i	ገጽ	page
gidigida	ግድግዳ	wall
gidiya	ግድያ	murder
gilits'i	ግልጽ	clear
gimashi	ግማሽ	half
giniboti	ግንቦት	May
gininyuneti	ግንኙነት	relationship
gīnit'i	ጊንጥ	scorpion
gira	ግራ	left
girach'a	ግራጫ	gray
girami	ግራም	kilogram
giši	ግሥ	**Verb**
gīzē	ጊዜ	time
gobet'e	ጎበጠ	bend
goma	ጎማ	tire
gorebēti	ጎረቤት	neighbor
gotete	ጎተተ	pull
gudati	ጉዳት	injury
gulibeti	ጉልበት	knee
gunich'ochu	ጉንጮቹ	**cheeks**
guridi k'emīsi	ጉርድ ቀሚስ	skirt
guridi koti	ጉርድ ኮት	jacket

guroro	ጉሮሮ	throat
gwadi	ጓድ	band
gwaniti	ጓንት	gloves
hābitami	ሀብታም	rich
ḫākīmi	ሐኪም	doctor
ḫākīmi bēti	ሐኪም ቤት	hospital
hāmilē	ሀምሌ	July
hamisa	ሃምሳ	fifty
ḫāmusi	ሐሙስ	Thursday
haya	ሃያ	twenty
haya - siminiti	ሃያ-ስምንት	twenty-eight
haya āmisiti	ሃያ አምስት	twenty-five
haya ānidi	ሃያ አንድ	twenty-one
haya ārati	ሃያ አራት	twenty-four
haya huleti	ሃያ ሁለት	twenty-two
haya sebati	ሃያ ሰባት	twenty-seven
haya sidisiti	ሃያ ስድስት	twenty-six
haya sositi	ሃያ ሶስት	twenty-three
haya zet'enyi	ሃያ ዘጠኛ	twenty-nine
ḫāyik'i	ሐይቅ	lake
ḫayili	ኃይል	energy
hayimanoti	ሃይማኖት	religion
hidari	ህዳር	November
ḫilimi	ሕልም	dream
ḫimemi	ሕመም	pain
hinits'a	ሕንፃ	building
ḫīsabu	ሂሳቡ	bill
ḫits'ani	ሕፃን	child
ḫits'ani	ሕፃን	child

hits'ani liji	ሕፃን ልጅ	baby
hiwasi	ሕዋስ	cell
hizibi	ሕዝብ	people
hizibi	ሕዝብ	crowd
hodi	ሆድ	stomach
hotēli	ሆቴል	hotel
huletenya	ሁለተኛ	second
huleti	ሁለት	two
ibabi	እባብ	snake
ich'u	እጩ	candidate
idifi	እድፍ	stain
igiri	እግር	foot
igiri	እግር	leg
īgiwana	ኢጓና	iguana
ihiti	እህት	sister
ihudi	እሁድ	Sunday
iji	እጅ	hand
inati	እናት	mother
inē	እኔ	I
inesu	እነሱ	They
inesuni	እነሱን	Them
inich'eti	እንጨት	wood
īnichi	ኢንች	inch
inidemini āderiki	እንደምን አደርch	good morning
inik'ilifi	እንቅልፍ	sleep
inik'ulali	እንቁላል	egg
inisisati	እንስሳት	Animals
inya	እኛ	we
irati	እራት	dinner

irefiti	እረፍት	break
irisasi	እርሳስ	pencil
irisha	እርሻ	farm
irisiwa	እርስዋ	she
irisu	እርሱ	he
irit'ibi	እርጥብ	wet
irobi	እሮብ	Wednesday
isati	እሳት	fire
isike	እስከ	up
isike	እስከ	up
isiri bēti	እስር ቤት	prison
iyadege	እያደገ	grow
jeliba	ጀልባ	boat
jīnisi	ጂንስ	jeans
joro	ጆሮ	ear
k'ebeto	ቀበቶ	belt
k'ech'inē	ቀጭኔ	giraffe
k'ech'ini	ቀጭን	thin
k'edada	ቀዳዳ	hole
k'elebeti	ቀለበት	ring
k'elemi	ቀለም	color
k'elemi	ቀለም	paint
k'elet'e	ቀለጠ	melt
k'eni	ቀን	date
k'eni	ቀን	day
k'enyi	ቀኝ	right
k'ēsi	ቄስ	priest
k'et'i yale	ቀጥ ያለ	straight
k'eyi	ቀይ	red
k'ibati	ቅባት	cream

k'ibē	ቅቤ	butter
k'idamē	ቅዳሜ	Saturday
k'iribi	ቅርብ	near
k'it'eli	ቅጠል	leaf
k'its'ilochini	ቅጽሎችን	adjectives
k'obi	ቆብ	cap
k'oda	ቆዳ	skin
k'ofere	ቆፈረ	dig
k'ome	ቆመ	stand
k'onijo	ቆንጆ	beautiful
k'oret'e	ቆረጠ	cut
k'uch'i	ቁጭ	sit
k'ulifi	ቁልፍ	key
k'ulifi	ቁልፍ	lock
k'urach'i	ቁራጭ	piece
k'urisi	ቁርስ	breakfast
k'usawī	ቁሳዊ	material
k'ushasha	ቁሻሻ	dirty
k'ut'irochi	ቁጥሮች	numbers
kamēra	ካሜራ	camera
kaporiti	ካፖርት	coat
karidi	ካርድ	card
karita	ካርታ	map
kebadi	ከባድ	heavy
kefi yale	ከፍ ያለ	high
kēki	ኬክ	cake
keniferi	ከንፈር	lip
kenitība	ከንቲባ	mayor
k'enyi	ቀኝ	right

kese'āti	ከሰአት	afternoon
ketema	ከተማ	city
ketema	ከተማ	town
kibebi	ከበብ	circle
kifeti	ከፈት	open
kifili	ከፍል	room
kinidi	ከንድ	arm
kinidi	ከንድ	elbow
kinifi	ከንፍ	wing
kiremiti	ከረምት	winter
kīsi	ኪስ	pocket
kokebi	ኮከብ	star
komipiyuteri	ኮምፒዩተር	computer
korebita	ኮረብታ	hill
kwasi	ኳስ	ball
labi	ላብ	sweat
lami	ላም	cow
lami	ላም	cow
lapitopi	ላፕቶፕ	laptop
lelīti	ለሊት	night
lemegizati	ለመግዛት	buy
lemegizati	ለመግዛት	buy
lesilasa	ለስላሳ	soft
libi	ልብ	heart
libisi	ልብስ	clothing
libisi	ልብስ	dress
liyu liyu	ልዩ ልዩ	miscellaneous
lomī	ሎሚ	lemon
ma'ibeli	ማዕበል	wave

ma'izeni	ማዕዘን	corner
magibati	ማግባት	marry
maginyeti	ማግኘት	find
maḥiberi	ማኅበር	society
makisenyo	ማክሰኞ	Tuesday
malefi	ማለፍ	pass
maleti	ማለት	mean
manika	ማንካ	spoon
masebi	ማሰብ	think
mashenefi	ማሸነፍ	win
masitawesha	ማስታወሻ	note
masitemari	ማስተማር	teach
mat'ebi	ማጠብ	wash
mazorīya	ማዞሪያ	turn
mebilati	ሙብላት	eat
mebirati	ሙብራት	lamp
mebirati	ሙብራት	light
medabi	ሙዳብ	copper
medebiri	ሙደብር	store
medihanīti	ሙድሃኒት	drug
medihanīti	ሙድሃኒት	medicine
megabīti	ሙጋቢት	March
megenibati	ሙገንባት	build
megideli	ሙግደል	kill
megwagwazha	ሙጓጓዣ	transportation
mek'ut'erīya	ሙቁጠሪያ	meter
mekefati	ሙከፋት	sad
mekifeli	ሙከፈል	pay
mekīna	ሙኪና	car

mekīna	መኪና	engine
mekīna	መኪና	engine
melibesi	መልበስ	wear
melimeja	መልመጃ	exercise
memari	መማር	learn
memet'eni	መመጠን	measurement
memitati	መምታት	beat
memoti	መሞት	die
menafesha	መናፈሻ	park
menageri	መናገር	speak
menigedi	መንገድ	road
menigedi	መንገድ	street
menigišite semayati	መንግሥተ ሰማያት	heaven
menorīya bēti	መኖሪያ ቤት	home
menorīya bēti	መኖሪያ ቤት	apartment
menorīya bēti	መኖሪያ ቤት	flat
menyita bēti	መኝታ ቤት	bedroom
meramedi	መራመድ	walk
merēti	መሬት	earth
merēti	መሬት	ground
merifē	መርፌ	needle
merikebi	መርከብ	ship
merizi	መርዝ	poison
mešaferīya	መዛፈሪያ	station
mesali	መሳል	draw
mesami	መሳም	kiss
mešarīya	መሣሪያ	instrument
mešarīya	መሣሪያ	tool
meshekemi	መሸከም	carry
meshet'i	መሸጥ	sell

mesikeremi	መስከረም	September
mesikoti	መስኮት	window
met'at'ebīya kifili	መጣጠቢያ ክፍል	bathroom
met'ifo	መጥፎ	bad
mets'iḫāfi	መጽሐፍ	book
mets'iḫēti	መጽሔት	magazine
mewanya	መዋኛ	pool
meweriweri	መወርወር	throw
meyazha	መያዣ	easel
mezigebe k'alati	መዝገበ ቃላት	dictionary
mi'irabi	ምዕራብ	west
migibi	ምግብ	food
migibi	ምግብ	feed
migibi	ምግብ	food
migibi bēti	ምግብ ቤት	restaurant
milasi	ምላስ	tongue
milikiti	ምልክት	sign
mīlīyoni	ሚሊዮን	million
minich'i	ምንጭ	spring
minich'i	ምንጭ	spring
mirich'a	ምርጫ	election
misa	ምሳ	lunch
mishiti	ምሽት	evening
misili	ምስል	image
misirak'i	ምስራቅ	east
mīsiti	ሚስት	wife
mīyazīya	ሚያዚያ	April
mīzani	ሚዛን	weight
moti	ሞት	death

muk'eti	ሙቀት	heat
muk'i	ሙቅ	hot
muk'i	ሙቅ	warm
mulu libisi	ሙሉ ልብስ	suit
muzi	ሙዝ	banana
muzīk'a	ሙዚቃ	music
nech'i	ነጭ	white
nefasi	ነፋስ	wind
nege	ነገ	tomorrow
negerefeji	ነገረፈጅ	lawyer
neḥāsē	ነሐሴ	August
neka	ነካ	touch
neširi	ነሥር	eagle
net'ibi	ነጥብ	dot
nigišiti	ንግሥት	queen
niguši	ንጉሥ	king
nits'uhi	ንጹሕ	clean
nukilīyeri	ኑክሊየር	nuclear
pami	ፓም	apple
pawunidi	ፓውንድ	pound
pilasitīki	ፕላስቲክ	plastic
pirēzīdaniti	ፕሬዚዳንት	president
pirogirami	ፕሮግራም	program
polīsi	ፖሊስ	police
radīyoni	ራዲዮን	radio
rasi	ራስ	head
rejimi	ረጅም	long
rejimi	ረጅም	tall
rek'īk'i	ረቂቅ	abstract
rikashi	ርካሽ	cheap

ruch'a	ሩጫ	run
ruk'i	ሩቅ	far
ruzi	ሩዝ	rice
šahini	ሳህን	plate
sak'i	ሳቅ	laugh
saminiti	ሳምንት	week
samuna	ሳሙና	soap
sanitīmētiri	ሳንቲሜትር	centimeter
šari	ሣር	grass
sat'ini	ሳጥን	box
sayinisi	ሳይንስ	science
še'alī	ሠዓሊ	artist
se'ati	ሰዓት	clock
se'āti	ሰአት	hour
seba	ሰባ	seventy
sebati	ሰባት	seven
šeferi	ሠፈር	camp
sefī	ሰፊ	wide
sek'ele	ሰቀለ	hang
selami	ሰላም	peace
selasa	ሰላሳ	thirty
seleba	ሰለባ	victim
sema	ሰማ	hear
semaniya	ሰማንያ	eighty
semayawī	ሰማያዊ	blue
semayi	ሰማይ	sky
semēni	ሰሜን	north
senē	ሰኔ	June
senyo	ሰኞ	Monday

serigi	ሰርግ	wedding
sēti	ሴት	female
sēti	ሴት	woman
sēti āyati	ሴት አያት	grandmother
sēti liji	ሴት ልጅ	girl
sēti liji	ሴት ልጅ	daughter
sēti liji	ሴት ልጅ	girl
sewi	ሰው	man
sewi	ሰው	person
shayi	ሻይ	tea
shekila	ሸክላ	clay
shelek'o	ሸለቆ	valley
shemīzi	ሸሚዝ	shirt
shiniti bēti	ሽንት ቤት	toilet
shita	ሽታ	smell
shoriba	ሾርባ	soup
sī'oli	ሲኦል	hell
sidisiti	ስድስት	six
sikirīni	ስክሪን	screen
siliki	ስልክ	phone
siliki	ስልክ	telephone
silisa	ስልሳ	sixty
simimineti	ስምምነት	contract
simiti	ስምት	eight
šine t'ibebi	ሥነ ጥበብ	art
sīnī	ሲኒ	cup
siporiti	ስፖርት	sport
šira	ሥራ	Job
šira	ሥራ	work
šira	ሥራ	job

širi	ሥር	root
sit'ota	ስጦታ	gift
sositi	ሶስት	three
sukari	ሱካር	sugar
surī	ሱሪ	pants
t'a'iti	ጣዕት	taste
t'ara	ጣራ	ceiling
t'ara	ጣራ	roof
t'ati	ጣት	finger
t'atochi	**ጣቶች**	**fingers**
t'ebabi	ጠባብ	narrow
t'ebabi	ጠባብ	tight
t'ebenija	ጠበንጃ	gun
t'eguri	ጠጉር	hair
t'ēnama	ጤናማ	healthy
t'ēnama	ጤናማ	sound
t'enikara	ጠንካራ	hard
t'enikara	ጠንካራ	strong
t'erep'ēza	ጠረጴዛ	table
t'erimuzi	ጠርሙዝ	bottle
t'erizi	ጠርዝ	edge
t'et'a	ጠጣ	drink
t'ewati	ጠዋት	morning
t'ik'ati	ጥቃት	attack
t'ik'imiti	ጥቅምት	October
t'ik'uri	ጥቁር	black
t'ik'uri	ጥቁር	dark
t'ik'uri	ጥቁር	dark
t'ileti	ጥለት	pattern

t'ilik'i	ጥልቅ	deep
t'ilik'i yalihone	ጥልቅ ያልሆነ	shallow
t'īmi	ጢም	beard
t'imizi	ጥምዝ	curved
t'iri	ጥር	January
t'irī	ጥሪ	call
t'irisi	ጥርስ	teeth
t'irisi	ጥርስ	tooth
t'iru	ጥሩ	cool
t'iru	ጥሩ	good
t'iru	ጥሩ	nice
t'ori šerawīti	ጦር ሠራዊት	army
t'orineti	ጦርነት	war
tachi	ታች	bottom
tahisasi	ታህሳስ	December
tarīki	ታሪክ	story
teba'iti	ተባዕት	male
tech'awachi	ተጫዋች	player
tegodahu:	ተጎዳሁ:	count
teketeli	ተከተል	follow
tekili	ተክል	plant
tēkinolojī	ቴክኖሎጂ	technology
tekose	ተኮሰ	shoot
tēlēvīzhini	ቴሌቪዥን	television
temarī	ተማሪ	student
temeliketi	ተመልከት	see
tenik'et'ek'et'e	ተንቀጠቀጠ	shake
terara	ተራራ	mountain
tewe	ተወ	stop
tewulat'e simi	ተዉላጠ ስም	pronoun

tī - tīsheriti	ቲ-ቲሸርት	T-shirt
ti'igišitenya	ትዕግሥተኛ	patient
tigili	ትግል	fight
tikesha	ትከሻ	shoulder
tīkēti	ቲኬት	ticket
tikusati	ትኩሳት	temperature
tilik'i	ትልቅ	big
tilik'i šat'ini	ትልቅ ሣጥን	chest
timihiriti bēti	ትምህርት ቤት	school
tinanitina	ትናንትና	yesterday
tinishi	ትንሽ	small
tiraki	ትራክ	truck
tiyatiri bēti	ትያትር ቤት	theater
ts'afe	ጻፈ	write
ts'eḫāfī	ጸሐፊ	secretary
ts'eḫāyi	ጸሐይ	sun
ts'eleye	ጸለየ	pray
ts'et'i yale	ጸጥ ያለ	quiet
vaweli	ቫወል	vowel
vuka	ቩካ	fork
waga	ዋጋ	price
wanye	ዋኘ	swim
wedeḫwala	ወደኋላ	back
wedeḫwala	ወደኋላ	back
wedek'e	ወደቀ	fall
wedetachi	ወደታች	down
wefi	ወፍ	bird
wefirami	ወፍራም	thick
wegeni	ወገን	side

wek'itawī	ወቅታዊ	seasonal
wek'iti	ወቅት	season
welaji	ወላጅ	parent
weleli	ወለል	floor
wemiberi	ወምበር	chair
wenidi āyati	ወንድ አያት	grandfather
wenidi liji	ወንድ ልጅ	boy
wenidi liji	ወንድ ልጅ	son
wenidimi	ወንድም	brother
wenizi	ወንዝ	river
werek'eti	ወረቀት	paper
weri	ወር	month
werik'i	ወርቅ	gold
werik'i	ወርቅ	gold
wet'ati	ወጣት	young
wet'i bēti	ወጥ ቤት	kitchen
wet'i bēti sēti	ወጥ ቤት ሴት	cook
wetaderi	ወታደር	soldier
weteti	ወተት	milk
wich'i	ውጭ	outside
widi	ውድ	expensive
wiha	ውሃ	water
wik'iyanosi	ውቅያኖስ	ocean
wisha	ውሻ	dog
wisikī	ውስኪ	whiskey
wisit'i	ውስጥ	inside
yak'at'ilewali	ያቃጥለዋል	burn
yaridi	ያርድ	yard
yašama šiga	ያሳማ ሥጋ	pork

yat'alu	ያጣሉ	lose
yaze	ያዘ	catch
ye'ālikoli met'et'i	የአልኮል መጠጥ	alcoholic drink
ye'ātikiliti	የአትክልት	garden
ye'āwiropilani marefīya	የአውሮፕላን ማረፊያ	airport
ye'igiri t'ati	የእግር ጣት	toe
yebahiri daricha	የባህር ዳርቻ	beach
yeberē šiga	የበሬ ሥጋ	beef
yederek'e āyibi	የደረቀ አይብ	cheese
yek'umi	የቁም	portrait
yekatīti	የካቲት	February
yemēda āhiya	የሜዳ አህያ	zebra
yemirich'a werek'eti	የምርጫ ወረቀት	ballot
yemote	የሞተ	dead
yemuzīk'a	የሙዚቃ	musical
yenya	የኛ	our
yesētochi shemīzi	የሴቶች ሸሚዝ	blouse
yeši'ili masaya ādarashi	የሥዕል ማሳያ አዳራሽ	gallery
yetameme	የታመመ	sick
yetē'ātiri tech'awachi	የቴአትር ተጫዋች	actor
yetē'ātiri tech'awachi	የቴአትር ተጫዋች	actress
yetefeta	የተፈታ	loose
yeweyini t'eji	የወይን ጠጅ	wine
yich'awetalu	ይጫወታሉ	play
yihi	ይህ	it
yimeliketu	ይመልከቱ	watch
yunīverisītī	ዩኒቨርሲቲ	university
zafi	ዛፍ	tree

zarē	ዛሬ	today
zefeni	ዘፈን	song
zelele	ዘለለ	jump
zemiru	ዘሙሩ	sing
zeri	ዘር	seed
zeri	ዘር	race
zeri	ዘር	race
zēro	ዜሮ	zero
zet'ena	ዘጠና	ninety
zet'enyi	ዘጠኝ	nine
zeyiti	ዘይት	oil
zigi yale	ዝግ ያለ	slow
zihoni	ዝሆን	elephant
zik'i yale	ዝቅ ያለ	low
zimibi	ዝምብ	fly
zinabi	ዝናብ	rain
zinijero	ዝንጀሮ	monkey
ziyī	ዝዬ	goose

መጽሐፍ ቅዱስ ከ የተመረጡ ቁጥር

በእርሱ የሚያምን ሁሉ የዘላለም ሕይወት እንዲኖረው እንጂ እንዳይጠፋ እግዚአብሔር አንድያ ልጁን እስኪሰጥ ድረስ ዓለሙን እንዲሁ ወዶአልና። - [፩ የዮሐንስ መልእክት 3:16]

ሁሉ ኃጢአትን ሠርተዋልና የእግዚአብሔርም ክብር ጎድሎአቸዋል፤ [ወደ ሮሜ ሰዎች 3:23]

የኃጢአት ደመወዝ ሞት ነውና፤ የእግዚአብሔር የጸጋ ስጦታ ግን በክርስቶስ ኢየሱስ በጌታችን የዘላለም ሕይወት ነው። - [ወደ ሮሜ ሰዎች 6:23]

ኢየሱስም። እኔ መንገድና እውነት ሕይወትም ነኝ፤ በእኔ በቀር ወደ አብ የሚመጣ የለም። - [፩ የዮሐንስ መልእክት 14:6]

ለተቀበሉት ሁሉ ግን፥ በስሙ ለሚያምኑት ለእነርሱ የእግዚአብሔር ልጆች ይሆኑ ዘንድ ሥልጣንን ሰጣቸው፤ - [፩ የዮሐንስ መልእክት 1:12]

ኢየሱስም መልሶ፡ እውነት እውነት እልሃለሁ፣ ሰው ዳግመኛ ካልተወለደ በቀር የእግዚአብሔርን መንግሥት ሊያይ አይችልም አለው። - [ኛ የዮሐንስ መልእክት 3:3]

እንደ ሕጉም ከጥቂቶች በቀር ነገር ሁሉ በደም ይነጻል፣ ደምም ሳይፈስ ስርየት የለም። - [ወደ ዕብራውያን 9:22]

እንዲህም አለ፡ እውነት እላችኋለሁ፣ ካልተመለሳችሁ እንደ ሕፃናትም ካልሆናችሁ፣ ወደ መንግሥተ ሰማያት ከቶ አትገቡም። - [የማቴዎስ ወንጌል 18:3]

እነሆ በደጅ ቆሜ አንኳኳለሁ፤ ማንም ድምፄን ቢሰማ ደጁንም ቢከፍትልኝ፣ ወደ እርሱ እገባለሁ ከእርሱም ጋር እራት እበላለሁ እርሱም ከእኔ ጋር ይበላል። - [የዮሐንስ ራእይ 3:20]

በኃጢአታችን ብንናዘዝ ኃጢአታችንን ይቅር ሊለን ከዓመፃም ሁሉ ሊያነጻን የታመነና ጻድቅ ነው። - [1 ኛ የዮሐንስ መልእክት 1:9]

ኢየሱስ ጌታ እንደ ሆነ በአፍህ ብትመሰክር እግዚአብሔርም ከሙታን እንዳስነሣው በልብህ ብታምን ትድናለህ፤ ሰው በልቡ አምኖ

ይጸድቃልና በአፍም መስክሮ ይድናልና። የጌታን ስም የሚጠራ ሁሉ ይድናልና። - [ወደ ሮሜ ሰዎች 10:9,10,13]

ጸጋው በእምነት አድኖአችኋልና፤ ይህም የእግዚአብሔር ስጦታ ነው እንጂ ከእናንተ አይደለም፤ ማንም እንዳይመካ ከሥራ አይደለም። - [ወደ ኤፌሶን ሰዎች 2:8,9]

እንደ ምሕረቱ መጠን ለአዲስ ልደት በሚሆነው መታጠብና በመንፈስ ቅዱስ በመታደስ አዳነን እንጂ፤ እኛ ስላደረግነው በጽድቅ ስለ ነበረው ሥራ አይደለም፤ - [ወደ ቲቶ 3:5]

እንርሱም። በጌታ በኢየሱስ ክርስቶስ እመን አንተና ቤተ ሰዎችህ ትድናላችሁ አሉት። - [የሐዋርያት ሥራ 16:31]

በልጁ የሚያምን የዘላለም ሕይወት አለው፤ በልጁ የማያምን ግን የእግዚአብሔር ቁጣ በእርሱ ላይ ይኖራል እንጂ ሕይወትን አያይም። - [ኛ የዮሐንስ መልእክት 3:36]

እኔም የዘላለም ሕይወትን እሰጣቸዋለሁ። ለዘላለምም አይጠፉም፤ ከእጄም ማንም አይነጥቃቸውም። - [ኛ የዮሐንስ መልእክት 10:28]

ስለዚህ ማንም በክርስቶስ ቢሆን አዲስ ፍጥረት ነው፤ አሮጌው ነገር አልፏልና፤ እነሆ፥ ሁሉም አዲስ ሆኖአል። - [2ኛ ወደ ቆሮንቶስ ሰዎች 5:17]

Selected Verses from the Bible

For God so loved the world, that he gave his only begotten Son, that whosoever believeth in him should not perish, but have everlasting life. - John 3:16

For all have sinned, and come short of the glory of God; - Romans 3:23

For the wages of sin is death; but the gift of God is eternal life through Jesus Christ our Lord. - Romans 6:23

Jesus saith unto him, I am the way, the truth, and the life: no man cometh unto the Father, but by me. - John 14:6

And said, Verily I say unto you, Except ye be converted, and become as little children, ye shall not enter into the kingdom of heaven. - Matthew 18:3

And I give unto them eternal life; and they shall never perish, neither shall any man pluck them out of my hand. - John 10:28

But as many as received him, to them gave he power to become the sons of God, even to them that believe on his name: - John 1:12

Jesus answered and said unto him, Verily, verily, I say unto thee, Except a man be born again, he cannot see the kingdom of God. - John 3:3

He that believeth on the Son hath everlasting life: and he that believeth not the Son shall not see life; but the wrath of God abideth on him. - John 3:36

And they said, Believe on the Lord Jesus Christ, and thou shalt be saved, and thy house. - Acts 16:31

That if thou shalt confess with thy mouth the Lord Jesus, and shalt believe in thine heart that God hath raised him from the dead, thou shalt be saved. For with the heart man believeth unto righteousness; and with the mouth confession is made unto salvation. For whosoever shall call upon the name of the Lord shall be saved. - Romans 10:9,10,13

For by grace are ye saved through faith; and that not of yourselves: it is the gift of God: Not of works, lest any man should boast. - Ephesians 2:8,9

Not by works of righteousness which we have done, but according to his mercy he saved us, by the washing of regeneration, and renewing of the Holy Ghost; - Titus 3:5

And almost all things are by the law purged with blood; and without shedding of blood is no remission. - Hebrews 9:22

Therefore if any man be in Christ, he is a new creature: old things are passed away; behold, all things are become new. - II Corinthians 5:17

If we confess our sins, he is faithful and just to forgive us our sins, and to cleanse us from all unrighteousness. - I John 1:9

Behold, I stand at the door, and knock: if any man hear my voice, and open the door, I will come in to him, and will sup with him, and he with me. -

Revelation 3:20

Sources Used

http://www.omniglot.com/writing/amharic.htm

www.sonofgod.net

http://learn101.org/amharic_nouns.php

http://www.effectivelanguagelearning.com/language-guide/amharic-language

https://en.wikipedia.org/wiki/Amharic

English translation of the Bible is from the King James Version.

The Amharic verses are from the version of 1962 [Old Version]. The Bible Society of Ethiopia is the owner of this Bible.

CPSIA information can be obtained
at www.ICGtesting.com
Printed in the USA
FSOW04n1054140616
21520FS